BLESSINGS

JOHN MICHAEL TALBOT

BLESSINGS

Reflections on the Beatitudes

CROSSROAD • NEW YORK

1991

The Crossroad Publishing Company
370 Lexington Avenue, New York, NY 10017

Printed in the United States of America
Typesetting output: TEXSource, Houston

Library of Congress Cataloging-in-Publication Data

Talbot, John Michael.
    Blessings : reflections on the beatitudes / John Michael Talbot.
        p. cm.
    ISBN 0-8245-1077-1
    1. Beatitudes—Devotional literature. I. Title.
BT382.T28 1991
241.5′3—dc20   90-41935
                                                         CIP

Contents

Introduction

Blessing! "God bless you." "May the Lord bless you." "May the blessing of almighty God come upon you." "May God bless ya real good!" We hear these "blessings" frequently in the various expressions of Christianity. But what does "blessing" really mean for the followers of Jesus Christ?

Some newer translations present the Greek word for "blessing" as "happy." True enough, the Greek word *macarius* is the same one used in naming a particular island, "The Happy Isle." So in some translations we have Jesus saying, "Happy are the poor in spirit" in the Beatitudes.

While the intent of this translation is correct, it has some serious problems in light of modern Western society. We are a people who aggressively and jealously claim "the pursuit of happiness" as our absolute right. While such a value is partially correct, it has been translated and interpreted to mean a society of "me-first" people. "Look out for number one," has become the byword for us upwardly mobile capitalists. We have become a materialistic people, a sexually perverse and promiscuous people, and a militaristic people all in the name of "happiness." We have made the philosophi-

7

cal, theological, and political justification of this self-centered happiness an art. But it does not make anyone truly happy. It causes poverty, war, and the breakdown of the whole human family, not to mention the breakdown of the essential unit of human existence — the nuclear family. It is, in the true sense of the word, sin.

Ironically, this "happiness" has been preached as the gospel of Jesus Christ in America and other nations of the West. Some prosperity churches paint Jesus' name all over materialism. Liberal churches paint his name on the surface of their loose sexual morality. Others make a giant step backward into the Hebrew Bible to justify their violence, racism, and militancy. All of them are doing only one thing: making a "gospel" of self-centeredness and a "blessing" of this self-centered happiness. These "gospels" are, as Paul said, "another gospel." These "blessings" do not bring good news. They bring bad news.

This is not the intent of the word "blessings." The "Happy Isle" is blessed because it remains tranquil and at peace despite the storms and troubles of the world. Such tranquillity doesn't mean there will be no cause for self-sacrifice. It doesn't mean there will be no storms or struggles. It simply means that, through it all, there will remain a deep and abiding "happiness" that cannot be changed by the struggles and turmoils of our world.

Of course, the central teaching of Jesus Christ regarding "blessedness" is found in the Beatitudes. These teachings are central to our faith. They form the core of Jesus' teaching in the Sermon on the Mount. They are the heart of the New Covenant. It has been said that, as the Ten Commandments are to the whole Law in the

Hebrew Bible, so the Beatitudes are to the entire New Testament.

It is obvious that they speak of a way of life radically different from the self-centered, me-first pursuit of happiness so widely accepted in the developed nations of the West. They speak of poverty, mourning, meekness, righteousness, mercy, purity of heart, peacemaking, and being persecuted as the way to real "blessing." They stand in radical opposition to the world in which we find ourselves. But they still remain the way of salvation for the whole world.

The way of the Beatitudes is the way of opposites. It is the way of mystery. The way of love. It makes sense only if you understand the love that is willing to sacrifice the self for the sake of another . . . for the sake of God . . . for the sake of all humankind as a whole and for the sake of each individual soul. Indeed, for the sake of all creation. This is the way of God's love that brings the real happiness and blessing that lasts for an eternity.

This is the way of the cross. The cross, where logic gives way to paradox, and paradox paves the way for love. It is here that a truth greater than the mind or the senses can be set free. It is here that the depths of the human soul assent to the greatest of all truths and happiness — the way of love.

What is this way? It is where we find wealth in poverty, deeper joy in sorrow, glory in meekness, wholeness in righteous holiness, justice in mercy, clarity in purity of heart, equality in peacemaking, and final victory even in persecution. This is a way that confronts the logic of the mind. It speaks directly to the heart and soul. It seems to be a contradiction, yet it remains forever true.

This little book is simply a devotional reflection on the blessings found in the Beatitudes. It is the result of much research and study, but it is not intended to be a scholarly book itself. I wrote this book almost existentially as a spontaneous overflow from my own personal prayer and study, from my own meditation on the Beatitudes of Jesus Christ. I hope you find it helpful.

It has been said that my music reflects Jesus, while my preaching and writing reflect Paul. And some have even said they reflect John the Baptist! While I am honored by and unworthy of any such comparisons, I must admit my heart longs after the way of Jesus. It is my hope that this simple and humble sharing of my own thoughts and prayers will overflow from Jesus to lead others back to Jesus and Jesus alone. The world is at an hour that needs him more than ever before.

The 1990s are being called the decade of evangelization. This is the decade of decision. We face challenges within the world that will decide the future of civilization as we know it. The problems seem overwhelming. But this is a time for hope. Yes, the problems might be immense. To ignore them would be untrue. But we have answers in Jesus Christ and in the church. As the world seems to be struggling in the curse, this is a time to bring forth blessing.

1

*"When he saw the crowds,
he went up the mountain,
and after he had sat down,
his disciples came up to him.
He began to preach."*

So BEGINS THE SERMON ON THE MOUNT. So begin the Beatitudes. It would be easy to gloss over these words and jump right into the first Beatitude. But this would be a great mistake. There is much in these opening verses that provides an essential introduction to the words by way of actions. It is an introduction by way of sign and symbol.

The prophets before Jesus were accustomed to using signs and symbols in the delivery of the word of the Lord. Samuel used the tearing of his tunic to prophesy the tearing of the kingdom away from King Saul (1 Sam. 16:27–29). Isaiah used the conception and birth of his own son as a symbol in a prophesy about the triumphs of one kingdom over another (Isa. 8:1–4). Ezekiel, likewise, used signs and symbols, as well as words, to communicate the word of the Lord (Ezek. 12, 21, etc.).

Indeed, the Middle Eastern mind understands sign and symbol as clearly as it understands the spoken word. Likewise, it understands analogy and parable almost better than the clear proclamation of objective truth and fact.

Jesus himself rarely taught through the objective use of Scripture and fact. He taught by way of analogy and parable far more than he objectively used Scripture or cold, philosophical truth. He appealed to the lily of the field, the birds of the air, or the grain of wheat to teach the greater and deeper truths of the reign of God. Likewise, he used the lessons of common, everyday humanity to teach the things of divinity. All of creation became for him a book of holy doctrine and a proclamation of the word of God. Furthermore, his ministry of healing the sick and exorcising demons taught far more of God's reign by action than he ever could through a ministry of mere words.

Why is this so? The sign and symbol, the parable and analogy, proclaim not only fact. They also proclaim mystery. They state what can be said through philosophical speculation, plus much more! They proclaim a world of reality that is beyond objective reason. They proclaim a truth that can be perceived only through the patient experience of life and the yearnings of the human heart. Yet they remain the deeper truths of human existence. They remain the deeper truths of the living word of God.

All this is of vital importance in light of one overwhelming fact: The majority of the world is of the same mind as the Middle Eastern world was in the time of Christ. It is Oriental. We, on the other hand, are Western. We are Occidental. In fact, most of Christianity has developed as a Western religion. In order to reach that Oriental world with the message of Christ, we must rediscover the teaching method of Christ himself, the method of sign and symbol, the weaving of parables and stories, the mystery of an action and analogy, rather than the repeated use of cold and lifeless words.

It should also be at least noted that Christianity has largely become a religion of the West. It is Occidental. It has become a religion of highly developed doctrine and objective truth. This happened as the faith spread from the Middle East into the places and times of the empires and dominations of the West. Consequently, the language of this Western Christian faith became increasingly logical and philosophical, with only a dogmatic use of Scripture at best. As a result, the mystery of faith was lost for the masses. Ironically, we lost the deeper truths of Scripture by an excessively logical use of Scripture. More importantly, by our dogmatic insistence on the truth of Jesus Christ, we lost the meaning that Jesus himself gave to Scripture. While this highly developed theology in the West can be a gift, it also threatens to alienate us from the very Christ we preach.

Christianity is not the fastest growing religion on earth. Islam is! Why? I believe it has a lot to do with the fact that it is an Oriental religion that is easily understood by a largely and increasingly Oriental world. It is able to supply simple and clear answers to life's questions, but in a way that fully takes mystery and paradox into account through the heavy use of parables. This approach is not lacking in Christianity. In fact, we possess it more than any other religion, but we must rediscover it in the person of Jesus Christ.

If we are going to rediscover the way of Jesus Christ, we must rediscover the power of sign, symbol, and parables. In this we will find ourselves more able to represent the Oriental worldview that Jesus shared, and more able to reach an increasingly Oriental world. The West is in decline. The East is on the rise. If we are going to reach both with the fullness of the gospel, we must rediscover the truly Middle Eastern Christ. We must rediscover the way of sign and symbol. Jesus is teaching us already before he has even opened his mouth.

"When he saw the crowds, he went up the mountain." What do these actions symbolize? If his actions speak through sign and symbol, what is Jesus saying here? Is this a deliberate choice, or the simple human response to a given situation? Probably a little of both. Yet these actions still speak loudly to very real human situations.

For me this action speaks of the paradox of "solitude and communion." It speaks of the relationship between prayer and action. Jesus goes up the mountain after seeing the crowds. But why? It is like bringing water to those in the desert. First, we must ourselves fill up our canteens in the oasis where there are abundant springs of water. Only then will we have anything to offer the thirsting souls when we find them. Then we can lead them back to the oasis where they can fill up canteens for themselves.

On one hand it could be argued that Jesus was seeking a spot away from the crowd so that he could pray and think. Only then would he really be able to minister to the crowd in the authentic power of the Spirit.

Jesus was a man of solitude. He knew how to fill up his canteens at the oasis of living water. He was born into the world away from the crowded inn in the solitude of a shepherd's cave. After his birth he was taken away from the tumult of Herod and into the solitude of Egypt and the desert. After his baptism he was led by the Spirit into the solitude of the desert of Judea to prepare for his ministry. During his ministry he was in solitude before preaching his great Sermon on the Plain, before choosing the Twelve, before the Transfiguration, and before the climax of his whole earthly ministry — the Passion. As Luke's Gospel says, "He often retired to deserted places and prayed" (Luke 5:16)

But his apparent solitude did not mean that he was totally alone. No! He usually took others with him into solitude. He was born in a solitary stable while "in community" with his mother, Mary, and his stepfather, Joseph. He was taken into the solitude of the desert of Egypt by Mary and Joseph.

Jesus was close enough to call his disciples after his solitary night of prayer before the choice of the Twelve. He was on a mountain, not far from the multitudes, before he preached the Sermon on the Plain. He actually took Peter, James, and John with him when he went into solitude from the rest of the Twelve on the mount of Transfiguration. Likewise, when he separated himself from the Twelve before the Passion, he took Peter, James, and John with him into his most agonizing experience of prayer. Yes, Jesus needed solitude for prayer, but he also chose to live in close communion with others.

Even in the human solitude of the desert during his temptation, he was joined by the Spirit from his heavenly Father, and by his adversary, the devil. We are never really alone. We are always surrounded by a "cloud of witnesses" (Heb. 12:1), even in the midst of our human solitude.

What does all this say? That we need to spend time in solitude and prayer before we attempt to evangelize others. We cannot evangelize until we have been evangelized. This happens most powerfully through solitary prayer. But it also says that even in living this life of prayer, we still need the support of others who are interested in the same thing. We cannot do it alone. We need help. Ironically, most of us cannot even go into solitary prayer without the support of other like-minded brothers and sisters. This is the lesson of Jesus' example.

But this is not the only lesson. Did Jesus go up the mount only to pray? I do not think so. I think Jesus went up that mountain in order to reach the people more effectively.

We can learn much from a simple visit to the traditional site of the Sermon on the Mount. It is not really much of a mountain. It is one of the higher hills directly on the north shore of the Sea of Galilee where Jesus did so much ministering. If he had been interested in prolonged solitude, he would have, doubtlessly, gone deeper into the mountains and hills. If you go to the top of that hill and speak in a loud, preaching voice, you can be heard all the way to the bottom! It is a phenomenon

of nature. I believe Jesus was making use of the natural surroundings in order to minister to the people. He
was not trying to avoid them. He did a similar thing
just to the east of this site, where he put out a short distance from the shore in a boat and spoke to the crowd
who were situated in a kind of natural amphitheater.
He used the natural tools at his disposal to reach the
crowds more effectively with his supernatural message.
Perhaps Jesus went up that mountain not so much to get
away from the crowd, but to do the exact opposite. Perhaps he went up that mountain in order to reach the
crowd more effectively.

So we see in Jesus' going up the mountain in response
to the crowd a double lesson, taught by example, taught
by sign and symbol. First, you need solitude before you
can minister to a crowd. You also need the support of a
like-minded, praying community before you can go out
to minister alone. And believe me, as soon as you open
your mouth to speak to a crowd, you are alone! Second,
we must meet the needs of the multitudes with both
supernatural and natural tools. We must not be afraid
to use natural things, such as P.A. systems, amphithe-
aters, or the perfect acoustics of a natural spot in order to
preach to the people — be it through example or word.
Likewise, we must be willing to use mundane things like
food, clothing, shelter, and medical supplies to preach
the good news of Jesus Christ. God works through all
the world in order to reveal the fullness of heaven.

Finally, this verse says to me: If you are afraid of
solitude, do not enter into community; and if you are
afraid of community, do not enter into solitude. Love
demands that neither solitude or community be an es-

cape from the real responsibility of relationship with and in Christ. Sometimes we run from Jesus and Jesus alone through "Christian" work. Sometimes we run from Jesus in others through "holy" solitude.

Furthermore, you cannot give what we do not have, we cannot evangelize others until God has evangelized us. But once we have this gift, we must always be ready to give it away as a gift to others. Never keep it only for yourself.

"After he had sat down, his disciples gathered around him." These words are also filled with powerful sign and symbol, perhaps even more than anywhere else in the New Testament except at the institution of the sacrament of Eucharist and in the Passion of Christ himself. It is the symbol of these actions that makes the Beatitudes themselves so central to the Sermon on the Mount and the entire New Testament.

The teachers of the Middle East did not stand. They sat. To teach from a seated position was a symbol of teaching authority. This is why Jesus said to respect the office of the Pharisees, even though we are not to follow their personal example. They sat upon the seat of Moses! (Matt. 23). Likewise, the synagogue leaders sat in a special seat in the assembly, higher than the rest. By taking a seated position before he taught the Beatitudes, Jesus was sending out strong signals, loud and clear, about his authority to teach and the importance of his words.

But the location of this "seat of authority" was also important. It was on a mountain. It was not in a synagogue, even though Jesus did teach in the synagogue. Nor was it in the Temple at Jerusalem, though he also taught in the Temple. No! This mountain was outside of the normal areas of the institutional religion of the Jews. It was in the open air. It was in the midst of unimpaired nature. It was something new!

Likewise, this teaching authority knew nothing of the institutional securities of either the local synagogue or the Temple in Jerusalem. It was wide open. It was vulnerable. It was poor. This new "church" was constituted by an itinerant rabbi, his disciples, and a multitude that followed him from place to place. They had no stable form of income. They often slept in the open air. Jesus himself had to perform a miracle on several occasions just to keep them fed, not to mention the paying of the Temple tax. No. This was no nice and secure community rising up neatly within the normal ranks of Judaism. It did not fit comfortably into the riches and glories of Solomon's Temple. It could not be confined by a synagogue wall. It was poor. It was unencumbered and free. It was to be radical and new!

But this symbol also built on the old. Jesus sat to teach "on a mountain." What does the mountain symbolize?

As we have already suggested, the mountain symbolized a "holy place." All through the Middle East the "high places" were seen as places of prayer and sacrifice for all the religions of the region. They became the solitary dwelling places for the various "schools of prophets" and priests. While the Jews were not to join in the pagan rituals and frequent the pagan high places, they too sought out high places of their own to worship the one true God. They too had prophets and priests who sought the solitude of these isolated and lofty mountains. The mountain stands as a symbol of the sacred and the holy.

But more importantly, the mountain stands as a symbol of the giving of the Covenant, the giving of the Law. It was upon Sinai and Horeb that Moses heard God's voice and was given the Law. It was on Sinai that God promised to lead the people out from bondage in Egypt into a promised land of their own. It was the teaching from this mountain that became the very essence and primary guidance for the people of Israel. It became the heart of the Jews.

By sitting to teach with authority from the top of this mountain, Jesus is saying through action before he speaks a word that what he says will become the heart of this new spiritual movement. This became especially apparent to those who looked back on those "symbols" after his earthly ministry was over. What he says becomes the heart of a new Law. As the Ten Commandments were to the Law of the Old Covenant, so the Beatitudes are to the new Law of the New Covenant. It is the essence of our whole way of life! Their importance cannot be overemphasized, yet they are often totally overlooked by followers of Jesus Christ.

"His disciples gathered around him." Notice that Jesus does not just speak in some haphazard way to the crowd. He does not sow the seed of his word carelessly. Instead, he gathers disciples and chooses the Twelve from among them. They lived with him intimately for a substantial period of time. Then he sends those who are the closest to him out on mission. First the Twelve. Then the seventy-two. He chooses them personally and gives them a special anointing of the

Spirit. Then he commissions them for leadership in the churches.

But it was not enough just to be chosen, commissioned, and empowered. They had to draw close to Jesus in order to hear his words. They had to get close to Jesus before they could draw others to him. They had to listen before they could preach. They had to be learners before they could teach. Likewise, they could not understand his words if they were not close to his person. Isolated from the life of the Incarnate Word, the teachings of Jesus became just another philosophy. His words cannot be separated from him. The disciples lived with him, ate with him, traveled with him. They saw him tired. They saw him hungry. They saw him successful and defeated, accepted and rejected. It was all this that gave power to his words. It was not enough only to hear him. They had to draw near to him.

The Twelve and the seventy-two were given special places of leadership by Jesus. Yes, the early church continued to employ special leaders to succeed the apostles for certain ministries. Yes, this leadership has succeeded the apostles right down to us today. But this example of sign and symbol is not only for church leadership.

This example is for us all! Not only were the apostles and disciples sent forth to minister through word, miracle, and example to the whole world; all followers of Christ were. All of us "who profess the faith" (Mark 16–17) are called to join with the apostles and special disciples to bring the good news to the whole world with the convincing power of the Holy Spirit.

But this cannot happen unless we take the time to

draw close to Jesus. As St. James says, "Draw close to God, and he will draw close to you."

This can be done in many ways. Through prayer, through the Scriptures, and through the sacraments. It can be in solitude or in the midst of our brothers and sisters in community. It can be in the specific gathering of the church, or out in the midst of our secular world. It can be with people, or in communion with God through all creation.

We can draw close to Jesus in many ways, but we must get close to him personally if we are really to hear the heart of his words. We must draw close to the person of Jesus himself if we are really to understand the meaning of the Beatitudes. We can draw near to Jesus in a special way through his real presence to us in the Eucharist. The early church believed Jesus was really present under the form of bread and wine. Why is this so necessary? Why is it so special?

Yes, Jesus is "really present" to us in the word of Scripture and through the "body of Christ," the church. But the word in Scripture is only written. The perfect and infallible body of Christ comes to us under the form of sinful human beings. Jesus knew we had a real need for his continual presence in a touchable, incarnate way that remained without sin. This is what he gives to us in Eucharist: Jesus, under the form of the simple and humble elements of creation, a staple food and drink for nearly all humankind, yet without the sins of humankind. Jesus is present only if confected by the word of God, spoken through a human minister representing the whole church, yet without the coldness of written words alone or the obvious sins and imperfections of the people of God.

It takes the eyes of faith to see Jesus in Eucharist. He cannot be seen with the eyes of the flesh. Once he is seen there, then the Scriptures come alive and the church becomes a sinless, spotless bride. In fact, all creation explodes in the mystery of Christ's redemption, which is at once perceptible and beyond perception, knowable and unknowable. It is truth, yet mystery. It is perfect sacrament.

This is all true, not just because the Eucharist is the most perfect sacramental sign and symbol in the world. It is true because Jesus said it, Jesus instituted it, and the early church believed it. For us in modern times, it remains a wonderful way to continually draw near to the real presence of Jesus.

"And he began to teach them." Only after speaking through sign and symbol is Jesus ready to speak with words. Only after being the Incarnate Word himself is Jesus ready to speak the word to others.

For the Middle Easterner the spoken word is the extension of the human soul. Only after a soul has lived what it is going to speak does it have the right or authority to speak. Otherwise, it makes a mockery of its own soul.

Jesus does not teach what he has not first learned. He has learned from his Father in heaven. He has learned through the Spirit on earth. Furthermore, he has had almost thirty years of living the normal life as a carpenter, and supposedly a carpenter's son, to learn how to implement his "lofty" ideals into mundane, earthly existence. If he spoke to ordinary people, it was because he had first learned how to implement his supernatural teachings in ordinary life. Likewise, he could teach the mystics because he first dared to go into the solitude of the desert to try his own teachings in the mystical fire of silence. Now he can lift up his voice.

The gospel passage we are looking at indicates repetition. The Greek use of "teach" is in the imperfect tense, suggesting repetition. Jesus probably did not teach them only once. He probably taught the Beatitudes many times. We know that Luke presents a very similar teaching in his Great Discourse, or Sermon on the Plain. Likewise, Matthew has Jesus teaching the Lord's Prayer, or Our Father, in the Sermon on the Mount in Galilee, while Luke has him teaching it outside of Jerusalem before his Passion. Jesus probably taught all his sermons, parables, and prayers many times and in many places, changing them to meet the unique, particular circumstance in which he and the disciples found themselves. "Repetition is the mother of learning." So goes the old saying. No doubt, Jesus made use of this very real and time-tested principle.

The Scripture says that the Jews were to constantly teach their children the Law of the Lord. Whether sitting or lying down. Whether at rest or at work. They were to be constantly teaching the word of the Lord to their children. Jesus, no doubt, experienced this firsthand from Mary as a young child, and from Joseph as a young man. This was the ancient Jewish custom.

The early church also practiced this repetition. Timothy knew the Scriptures from his youth and was well acquainted with the personal teaching of Paul (1 Tim. 4:2). The "rich deposit of faith" came from a telling and retelling of the gospel of Jesus and the teaching of the apostles on how to implement it in daily life. And it came from constantly being around the real people who live this word as a living, breathing way of life.

We too must grow accustomed to the continual repetition of the teaching and living of the Christian faith. They will sometimes seem old and tiresome. We will sometimes have "itching ears" for some new philosophy or religion. But do not lose heart and do not be deceived! It is through this repetition that your soul stays clear. Even when it seems to be accomplishing nothing, it is doing a secret work in your soul. As the saying goes, "Seven days without the word of God makes one weak."

We are like athletes. If we stop doing the old, familiar workout in practice every day, our muscles will grow soft and flabby. They will not be ready for the real contest when it comes. Likewise with the teachings of Jesus and Christianity. We may have heard them often. We may grow tired of doing our daily "spiritual exercises." But do not stop. If you do, your spiritual "muscles" will grow weak, and you will not be ready for the contest when it comes. And the contest is coming! It comes to all of us in different ways. It comes when we least expect it. Be prepared. Practice daily. Turn the stories of Jesus and the Christian faith in your heart and mind over and over. Do not grow tired of the repetition. As Paul says, "Do not grow weary of doing good." Do not let the contest catch you off guard!

2

"Blessed are the poor in spirit, for theirs is the kingdom of heaven"

Here JESUS BEGINS TO SPEAK. But he speaks in paradoxes. He has set himself up to preach the "new Law," and what does he speak? The pristine philosophy of the Greeks? The exposition of the Law? No! He speaks paradoxes — contradictions, riddles, nonsense!

But his listeners knew that his words were far from nonsense. Oh, yes, they seemed to be contradictions, but these paradoxes spoke apparent contradictions that remained true. They penetrated beyond the logic of the world and touched a divine spark of love and truth within the human soul.

Who were his listeners? Scribes, Pharisees, and religious leaders? Yes, they were watching and listening with careful scrutiny. The rich of the world? No doubt. The traders and wealthy merchants sought out this new "curiosity." Civil leaders? Yes. Rome was everywhere, watching for any sign of rebellion among this fanatically religious people. Yes, they were all there. But they were not the majority of Jesus' audience.

Most of this crowd were the poor. These were the *anawim*, God's "little ones." The poor laborers and workers who live hand to mouth from day to day. Along the seashore there were many fisherman as well, who made their living from the meager catch of the day. None of them were rich. All of them were highly taxed by Rome and by their own religious "Temple tax." They were the ever-present poor, forever working and never "getting ahead."

This is the lot that Jesus calls "blessed." What it must have done to their hearts to hear this prophet of God proclaim that they, not the rich secular or religious leaders, were the ones truly blessed by God! Did they understand it? Probably not. But they did know that this worker of God's miracles assured them that God did indeed care for them! This was a blessing enough in itself.

Jesus has much to say about the "backward logic" of gospel poverty. He says that we cannot be his disciples unless we renounce all our possessions. All of them! Not some. Not a few. Not all but a few. He says *all*. Why?

He says that we cannot serve both God and money. We will either love the one and hate the other, or hate the one and love the other. Both consume all and must be served by all. Is it literally all or nothing?

Likewise, he says that wherever your treasure lies, there will your heart be also. He does not say what we wish he had said: Where your heart is, there is your treasure. That is much more comfortable. That is easier to tolerate. No! He says that where our possessions are, there our hearts will be as well! Possessions have a strange way of stealing your heart.

But he also promises us that God will give us what we need in this world if we first renounce the world and seek only the kingdom of heaven. He says that he will, in fact, give us thirty or sixty or a hundred times as many things in this world if we will seek only the reward in heaven. He does not say that we will get back the hundredfold if we renounce things only to get more things. That isn't renunciation. That is accumulation!

He says that if we totally renounce the things of this earth in order to gain only heaven, then and only then will he make us stewards over more than we could possibly expect or imagine. If we totally give up everything, our possessions, our gifts, our talents, our earthly relationships, then he will put them back together in a way that wastes none of them, but uses them in a way we could never have even imagined.

We can see that this poverty affects not only external possessions, but internal attitudes. It affects the way we think and feel about things. This includes the way we use our natural gifts and talents.

Peter left his boats and nets to follow Jesus. Little could he know the full implication of what Jesus meant when he said, "Come after me and I will make you fishers of men." Because Peter let Jesus take him apart, Jesus was able to put Peter together in a whole new way. He used Peter's natural gifts and talents in a way that fulfilled them all, and, no doubt, surprised Peter completely! Peter gave up the little he thought he had, and gained everything on earth and in heaven in return. He gave up the care of his earthly family and gained the care of the entire family of God. He gave up his fishing in Galilee and gained a "net" he could throw out to all the peoples of the world.

I gave up the music I was trained for by the world. Jesus gave music back to me in a style I would never have come up with myself. I gave up family and friends, and Jesus gave me back a new family and friends — a church, a community, and a wife of whom I am not worthy or deserving. I gave up money and possessions, and now I am responsible for large amounts of money I could only dream of before, and none of which I now personally own.

God has blessed me beyond my wildest dreams. But this is only so because I gave up everything and sought only the reward of heaven. If I had sought possessions on earth, God would not have given them back to me. And if I try to possess them now, God will surely take them away.

On the level of personal relationships, we also must be "poor." We must be detached. If we try to possess other persons, they will never be free to be who God created them to be. Then the relationship will die. If we impose our ideas, our dreams, or if we try to control another person's development, then we run the risk of trying to make the other person in our image, rather than letting that person be conformed to the image of Christ. Of course, some direction is necessary from elders, and some sharing of dreams is healthy, but never at the cost of trying to possess another person.

This detachment involves an attitude of real humility. To see the legitimate gifts of God in another person and to allow God to prosper those gifts. To rejoice when those gifts prosper in another, even when we are not directly involved. Of course, every person on earth has a special gift from God, and when any one of them prospers, we all prosper. How tragic for all when we fail to let this process develop freely. How tragic when pride causes us to try to conform others to our image, rather than God's. How tragic when we try to possess our personal relationships. It always ends in failure for all.

If we "let go and let God" then all relationships prosper more than we could ever have imagined. They may not unfold as we expect or plan, but if we let them unfold according to God's will and plan, they truly bear the lasting good fruit of love, joy, and peace.

This poverty of spirit in relationships also involves our approach to obedience — obedience to God and obedience to others. St. Benedict says that this humility brings forth obedience to God through the leadership of the monastic community. St. Francis says that the true poverty of spirit spoken of in the Beatitudes of Christ is manifested through giving up our own opinion in minor matters and going along with the decision of our superior or community.

This kind of obedience is not some cold, legal principle. It is not a matter of law. It is a matter of the heart. It is a matter of love. This obedience is the result of a poverty of spirit that brings forth a humility that affects all our relationships with others, be they personal, communal, ecclesial, professional, or civil. Of course, in each of these levels, appropriate levels of honest dialogue are involved. And in major matters of faith and morality, we must follow our conscience. But through it all a very real humility and poverty of spirit will bring forth an obedience that is beautiful and free.

This obedience is not always easy. Jesus was obedient to God and others when he accepted death on a cross. But look at the results: Resurrection! Likewise, if we "die" to ourselves by embracing the poverty of obedience, then we will rediscover the wealth of resurrection in a way we could never see or guess or presuppose.

This kind of obedience is very difficult for the average American. We are programmed from youth to a whole different orientation. "I Did It My Way" is our theme song. "Independence" is our declaration. We have become a society of rugged individualists. This has given birth to a generation of people who want what they want, when they want it. Deference to others is simply not our style. "Look out for number one" has become the sad motto of an entire generation. Perhaps it will become our epitaph!

Our attitude stands in radical contrast to most of the world. Most of the world is more communal in its orientation. The community comes first, then comes the individual. The community serves the whole, which in turn benefits the individual. Sacrifice of self for the sake of the tribe or community is a given and accepted norm for most of the world. It is just the way it is done.

This can be seen (sometimes taken to an extreme) in many of the businesses of the Far East. They expect radical self-sacrifice and team effort in producing their product. This causes the whole business and, in turn, all the employees to prosper more quickly. Perhaps this is why the Orientals are quickly overtaking Westerners in financial success.

Likewise, the church is calling us to recognize the interdependence of all peoples and all creation. No one is really "independent" of other people or the laws of nature.

Likewise, dependency and codependency are proven to be unhealthy. Interdependence, where a group of healthy, confident people work together and sacrifice their own self-interests for the sake of the whole, is the standard that is quickly becoming even the secular norm for most of the world.

If we Americans are to keep pace with a rapidly changing world, we too must develop this attitude of interdependence. An appropriate and healthy obedience will soon follow. Consequently, we will have to rethink some of the essential American attitudes that in the final analysis stand in radical opposition to the reality of most of the population of the world and, even more importantly, to the Beatitudes of Jesus Christ. This is true, especially for Americans who profess to follow directly the way of Jesus Christ.

This hundredfold principle regarding internal attitudes, relationships, and possessions does not mean that actual external poverty is not important. It most certainly is! Matthew's Sermon on the Mount might well say, "Blessed are the poor in spirit." But Luke's Sermon on the Plain simply says, "Blessed are the poor." There can be no doubt that Jesus demanded actual external poverty of both himself and his disciples. Likewise, the only way safely to steward the reality of this hundredfold principle is to just keep giving it away. It becomes almost a holy competition with God.

In Christian history the physical expression of gospel

poverty has been lived out in three major ways. The first way is based on Matthew 10 and 19. It is a literal imitation of the itinerant poverty of Christ and his apostles. In this they owned nothing, either individually or even as a group. They had no place to rest their heads. They went from place to place to minister and relied entirely on the generosity of others for their basic needs of food, clothing, and shelter. The first way was adapted by St. Anthony of the Desert and the eremitical monks in the early church and rediscovered by St. Francis of Assisi and his mendicant friars in the fourteenth century. Today, it is practiced by some itinerant ministry teams and some lone pilgrims called by God.

The second way is based on Acts 2 and 4. In this the individuals voluntarily renounce personal ownership, and the community holds all things in common. This was practiced by the first church in Jerusalem as it tried to apply Jesus' radical teaching about poverty to the more stable life of raising a family in the city. It was also the pattern used by all cenobitical monks under the direction of St. Antony of Egypt, Pachomius of Egypt, St. Basil the Great in the later Christian East, and St. Benedict of Nursia in the West. Today, it is preached by almost all religious and monastic communities in the church, as well as by some radical lay communities being raised up by the Spirit of God.

The third way is based on 2 Corinthians 8. In this, individuals retain the right to private property, but share with those in need so that ideally a certain equality is achieved and maintained between the rich and poor of the church. This way was adapted as the church spread out to bring the radical gospel poverty of Jesus Christ to various civilizations of the world. It became the most widespread model in the early church, and — with the diaspora of the Jerusalem church of Acts 2 and 4 after the destruction of Jerusalem in 70 A.D. — it became the almost exclusive expression of gospel poverty for the average follower of Christ. Today, this way of equality with private ownership remains the primary expression of the average Christian.

But it must be seriously asked: Is there really equality? Is there really equality between the churches of the "developed North" and the "Third World?" Is there even equality between the rich suburban churches and the inner-city parishes in the developed world? Lastly, is there really equality between the "haves" and the "have nots" in any parish, rich or poor? I am afraid the answer is a definite and undeniable no. I am afraid to say that we are not even meeting the minimal standard of gospel poverty found in the New Testament.

This is a sad commentary on the "brotherly love" of Christianity, in America especially, when viewed against some simple facts: America represents only 6 percent of the world's population, but consumes 40 percent of the world's resources by even the most conservative estimate. Some say we consume 60 percent. Forty-two thousand people die every day of poverty-related causes. Forty thousand of those are children under the age of twelve. This means that over twenty million children could die of poverty and hunger-related causes in the 1990s alone. How ironic and challenging when the 1990s is supposed to be the decade to bring the good news of Jesus to the whole world. Obviously, things must change.

Right now, it is boasted by many that America gives more to the poor than any other nation on earth. But how much is this when compared to our total wealth? It is minimal!

Is this really the lesson of the widow's mite? Of all the developed nations of the earth, the United States gives less per person in foreign aid than any other. According to some studies, if every American were to give fifty cents a day, we would wipe out world hunger. But we are not even coming close. Our boastful statistics are not as true as they first appear.

Also for us to considered very seriously is the connection between poverty and war. When the minority of the "haves" continually oppress the "have nots," the "have nots" will eventually rise up and overthrow the "haves." It may take time, but it will happen. This continued materialism of the Christian West, therefore, becomes a major contributor to war and unrest. How totally inconsistent with the Beatitudes of Jesus Christ!

In light of the statistics of wealth and poverty and their relationship to population demographics, I would even say that we of the West are due to be overthrown. It may not happen violently. Because of God's mercy, it may happen through the gradual process of politics and economics. But it will occur. In fact, it has already begun.

The further tragedy of materialism is the death it causes to the materialistic. The more things we accumulate, the more thing-oriented we have to be, and the more thing-like we become. We lose our real humanity. Furthermore, the more we have, the more we want and the more dissatisfied we become. Materialism kills not only the poor it deprives. It kills the materialistic themselves. It causes a no-win scenario. The whole earth becomes the loser.

This materialism is nurtured and kept alive by "the beast." The beast is a system, sometimes even a religious system, that feeds on the very people and ideas it is supposed to save. It starts innocently enough. You produce a product that is good. Soon, more people want it. In order to produce more of the product, you hire more people and develop a growing infrastructure. Unfortunately, somewhere along the line you begin to sell the product in order to keep your infrastructure going. You even shear off quality in order to cut costs. Subtly, and without even knowing it, the focus of the business has changed from bringing a good thing to those in need to keeping sales up to support the infrastructure. Instead of serving people, it uses them. Instead of being centered on service, it is centered on the dollar.

Now we must all have a "beast." Even Christian ministries must employ some infrastructure in order to help bring their "product" to people in need. We all have light bills to pay. We also must support those who do the work of the ministry, either as employees or community members. But we can all keep the beast in a cage! How?

Perhaps something could be learned from the "pruning principle." This principle means that if you really want to see something bear lasting fruit in God's reign, it must be pruned. To prune means to cut back that which is not fruitful to send more strength to that which is. This process is sometimes painful. Sometimes it seems excessive. But it must be done if the tree is to bring forth abundant fruit.

By constantly pruning the tree of our ministry or business, we can keep the beast in a cage. We must constantly simplify our infrastructure if we do not want to let the beast out of the cage.

How desperately the world needs to see examples of gospel poverty today. Years ago Lenin said that if Russia had only ten St. Francises in its midst, there would not need to be a communist revolution. Today, we are seeing that neither Marxism nor capitalism really work. Today, we still need those St. Francises who will dare really to live the gospel poverty of Jesus Christ.

The first way of Matthew 10 and 19 is like a flash of lightning that lights up the sky with enough power to light a whole city in a matter of seconds. The second way of Acts 2 and 4 is like a great power station that harnesses that power to be put into practical use by millions. The third way of 2 Corinthians 8 is like the electric light bulb that can light a whole room for a long period of time.

How desperately we need those who will dare to follow the teaching of Christ and the early church. How desperately we need those who will dare take Jesus at his word.

Where are the St. Francises of our era? Where are the Simon Peters who will leave everything in order to bring the gospel to all? I will tell you where they are. They are reading these words right now. You are the ones. You are the St. Francises. You are the Simon Peters. You are the ones who have it within you to change the world for Christ in the last decade of this millennium. The question is... will you?

You start very simply. With every possession ask, "Is it a want or a need?" God wants to meet our needs, but God doesn't want us habitually to indulge our wants at the expense of the needy. St. Augustine said long ago, "When you indulge your wants you steal from the needy." Saint Francis said it hundreds of years later. And Gandhi said it from a non-Christian perspective in our own century. How sad it took a non-Christian to remind us of our own heritage in this regard!

So ask yourself, "Is it a want or a need?" God also wants us to take pleasure and joy in meeting our needs. God isn't interested in sullen and downcast "simple lives." But God does want us all to get serious about bringing joy to others by meeting their basic human needs. This means giving up our wants.

So there are two major gauges by which to get us going toward even the most permissive New Testament standard of gospel poverty. The first is: Live simply so others might simply live. The second is: Is it a want or a need? If we follow these two axioms, we will radically change the materialism of our personal lives.

But our approach to possessions affects individuals. It has corporate effects. It affects nations and empires. It affects economics and the environment of our whole planet. When individuals start demanding more and more "wants," then companies are formed to produce them. When the individuals of a society begin centering themselves on wants rather than needs, then the economic structure of that society will follow. Soon the economic structure of a whole society becomes centered

on producing "wants" rather than "needs." This has
vast ramifications. It places the whole society in a dangerous position indeed.

We are like a football player whose center of gravity
is too high. If he is hit, and most of them are sooner
or later, he will go flying. But if his center of gravity is
lower, when he gets hit he will have far less chance of
getting knocked down. Furthermore, when he sees a hit
coming, he gets lower and spreads wide.

Likewise with a society. If we allow our center of
gravity to get too high and away from our basic needs
by centering on our wants, then when we get econom-
ically hit, and most societies eventually do, we will go
flying wildly through the air and land violently on the
ground. If we keep our center of gravity low, around
our basic needs, then when we get hit we will have a
greater chance of staying on our feet.

What are these basic needs? Sirach says they are
food, clothing, and shelter. Paul, the itinerant, says that
if we have food and clothing we can be content. For a
stable model of society, Sirach's short list is more real-
istic.

Getting away from the production of these simple
needs has vast ramifications on the environment as
well. The following demographics will explain.

Before World War I, twenty-four out of every twenty-
five families in America lived on a farm. They produced
a real basic need: food, plus the wool and cotton used
in clothing. Only one out of twenty-five lived in the city
and produced specialized needs and occasional wants.

After World War II the demographics flip-flopped so
that only one out of every twenty-five families in Amer-

ica lived on a farm. Twenty-four out of twenty-five had moved to the city. Why? They no longer wanted to bear with the toil of tilling the soil all their lives. The lure of new industry tempted them with the opportunity for work less and make more money. Though not immediately apparent, the root cause was greed.

Today, only one out of fifty families lives on the farm. Forty-nine out of fifty live in the towns and cities of America. Consequently, we now have the majority of the population producing specialized wants for a want-oriented lifestyle. A minority of the population is left to produce our most basic needs: food.

What is the agricultural result of this change? Before, farms were small and crops were diversified. Each local area produced a majority of its basic needs. Only occasionally did people have to go to the city to buy a specialized need or want. Now, farms are huge. One family now farms what over forty families cared for before. Consequently, large machinery, chemical fertilizers, and pesticides must be used to keep up. Furthermore, only a few prime corps are planted. This means that the average American may go hundreds or thousands of miles to dinner every night! This means additional chemical preservatives must be used in order to keep the food fresh in travel and on the shelves.

All this is a hazard to the environment. It affects not only our natural environment, but the environment of our own bodies as well. The plague of the deadly killer cancer has been linked to the overchemicalization of our food and drink. Other sicknesses such as "environmental illness" (EI) result when the entire immunity system breaks down and one becomes literally allergic to everything. The causes: an oversaturization of artificial chemicals in the body through food and drink.

The ecology of the planet is another matter. "Spaceship earth" is in trouble. Our "lifeboat" has not only sprung a leak, it has a gaping hole. We are taking water fast! The artificial fixation of nitrogen in chemical fertilizers pollutes both our water and our ozone. It upsets the whole nitrogen cycle. This not only kills fish in the water and risks widespread damage to humans, but also the destruction of our ozone layer may have effects on weather so widespread we cannot even begin to guess them. Already, weather patterns seem more erratic and extreme. The hot is hotter. The cold is colder. Droughts, floods, and freezes hit more often and in unexpected places. What comes next, nobody really knows.

So the habitual indulging of our wants has widespread results. The results affect the poor. They affect world peace. They affect the spiritual, emotional, and physical health of human beings everywhere. Finally, they affect the environmental safety of the very planet we all live on. If we mess that up, there is nowhere else to go.

We can see that "poverty of spirit" has far-reaching effects. It changes internal attitudes that affect nearly every aspect of human life: personal and corporate relationships, all our possessions, our source of livelihood, sociopolitical and economic structures, and even the ecological balance of planet earth's environment.

In the final analysis, however, poverty of spirit brings us a "blessedness" that is beyond the ups and downs of our life in this troubled world. It brings a detachment from people, places, and things that in turn brings lasting internal peace. This is not a detachment devoid of love. It is a detachment inclusive of hope. Hope is a "reign of heaven" that lasts forever. Yes, it may break through and appear on earth from time to time through human efforts, but its lasting abode is only in heaven. Therefore, we work to bring God's reign on earth as it is in heaven, while we are still here. But through it all we know that this is not our lasting home. This is the poverty of spirit that builds up wealth in heaven that no one can take from us or steal. This is the poverty that offers lasting wealth to all.

3

"Blessed are they who mourn, for they shall be comforted"

AGAIN JESUS SPEAKS A TRUTH that is greater than the logic of the world. Again Jesus speaks a truth that breaks through to the hearts of his listeners. Who were they?

Most of these *anawim*, or little ones of God, lived a life that knew the reality of sorrow and mourning. The people of Israel were an oppressed nation, living under the tyranny of Rome. Even their own religious leaders laid heavy, legalistic burdens on their shoulders so that the very religion that should have brought them some comfort only drove them deeper into bondage. Oppression, sickness, and death were daily realities for those who struggled and toiled through life in a fishing and agricultural area of an insignificant province of the mighty Roman Empire.

But life was not all sadness and pain for the people of Galilee. They were a people who enjoyed the simple pleasures of life. The times of mourning and sadness only caused them to appreciate the good times even more. For many, the pain of sadness only served to pierce and sensitize their hearts. For some, however, the repeated pain and sorrow caused their hearts to grow calloused and cold. It was to avoid this latter condition that Jesus now spoke. He spoke to encourage. He spoke to give hope. He spoke to set the prisoners free.

But what about the modern followers of Christ? We face our own set of sorrows and afflictions. We may not live under military occupation, but we live in "occupied territory" just the same. A battle is being waged on every front. The struggles and trials of this world break in from every side. Many times it does not seem that we are always the "victorious in Christ." Jesus' words are just as much for us today as they were for that crowd of "little ones" in Galilee some two thousand years ago.

Are Christians always happy? Looking at today's "born again" churches in America, one could easily get that impression. The young, got-it-together, upwardly mobile Christians have a certain "look."

They smile all the time. Everything is always "fine," for it is in God's will. Life is always "good." Life is always upwardly mobile, for God wants us to "prosper," and if we do not prosper we are not really in God's will. The men are macho: straight-shouldered, worked-out, and tanned at the local health club. The women are similar: always made up, hair neatly in place, and clothes of the latest fashion.

Their language is full of "praise the Lord" and "thanksgiving" for their upwardly mobile, affluent lifestyle. In many ways we look more like yuppies for Christ than true disciples of Jesus Christ.

But underneath this façade of joy and happiness are

broken lives. This is the reality. Men who are scared and insecure about their position in this fast-paced, upwardly mobile society. Women who, despite all the cosmetics and health spa workouts, still think they are too fat or ugly. Beneath our model Christian families are divorces, broken homes, maladjusted children. Under the breath of the praises of God is cursing for the inner misery of typical American life. Behind the locked doors of our mansions and suburban homes are stacks of bills for the things we buy with credit cards and bank loans that we really cannot afford. Beneath the put-on smiles are tears, tears of real human sorrow. Sometimes our misguided or unbalanced Christian teaching actually represses that sorrow instead of redeeming it.

Jesus gives us an entirely different approach to sorrow. He redeems it. He makes it life-giving rather than a product of death, for Jesus has conquered death itself by redeeming it. Now it is through death that we find life. Likewise, it is through real human sorrow that we find divine joy.

At the beginning of Luke's story of Christ, Mary is called blessed but promised a sword. A sword pierces Mary's heart and she is called "blessed." Why? So many in our world have closed off their hearts. Perhaps it is because they have been hurt one too many times, and they simply put up a wall in self-defense like a callus around an overly sensitive wound. Perhaps it is because they were simply afraid to let anyone into their heart in the first place, so they shut everything out. Whatever the reason, this is a tragic reality in our modern world. People shutting everyone and everything out of their hearts, supposedly in order to save their lives, yet losing the fullness of life in the process.

It is the sword that pierces through all this to touch the heart again and wake it up. Does it hurt? It most certainly does. But it is the sword, it is the pain that resensitizes the heart to real human emotion again. It is often the pain that reminds the heart that it is still alive.

This pain is the price we pay for love. Love is a risk. It is not sorrow free. If we really love then we will hurt when another hurts. We will mourn when those we love suffer loss of any kind. We will grieve when they grow sick, become invalids, or die. We will grieve and mourn when our love is sometimes misunderstood or even rejected altogether. Love does not in any way guarantee that these experiences will somehow disappear from our lives. Therefore, if we dare to love, we will sooner or later experience pain. So the sword of pain comes from love. And love comes from God. Sometimes the sword of pain must be used by God to stir up love again.

Perhaps this is why the Scriptures say that if we want to find wisdom, do not enter into the house of joy. Enter into the house of sorrow. It is there we will often find tender and humble hearts. It is there we will often find the greatest wisdom about the most precious and lasting treasure of life.

It is also true that our faith is only as strong as it is at its weakest point. We find the weak points at times of tragedy. We find out how strong we really are in times of sorrow. Two things are true: We are usually not as strong as we think we are. At the same time, we are stronger than we ever dreamed possible. We never discover these revelations about ourselves and others unless we become vulnerable enough to experience and share our sorrow. This is the wisdom of the heart-piercing sword.

Life is both fragile and strong. It stands in an awesome balance between these two extremes. Yet both extremes are true. When these two realities are revealed to us, our hearts must explode with both sorrow and joy, rejoicing and mourning, in order to take it all in. When the sword that pierced Mary's heart finds its way into our hearts as well, there we find the greatest truths of our being by simply being reduced to tears. These tears are holy. This mourning is sacred. It is the way to lasting joy.

Sorrow is also holy because it leads to repentance. It brings us back to God. Like in the story of the prodigal son, when we see the misery of life away from the blessings of our heavenly Father, we feel sorrow and head back toward home. This is called "repentance."

What does repentance mean? To change. To turn around. To convert. Sorrow from discovering the sorry state of life without God leads to repentance. It leads to conversion. It causes us to turn around.

But sorrow is also an important part of the process once we have actually started the journey home. There are two kinds of repentance. One with sorrow. One without.

Repentance without sorrow is interested only in escaping the sorrow of the world. It is still interested only in itself. Yes, it turns toward God, but only as a logical escape from the sorrows of the world. It expects joy from now on.

Repentance with sorrow is also interested in escaping the sorrow of this world. But it is sorry because it has offended the heart of God, for love cannot center on the self. Repentance with sorrow is pleasing to God because it is a repentance of love. It is this kind of repentance that is truly blessed by God. It is this kind of repentance that is rich, wonderful, and full.

One kind of repentance is centered on self. The other is centered on God. One is a repentance of logic. The other is a repentance of love. One sees God as a solution to a problem. The other sees God as a personal and living God to be loved. Sorrow for sin is a test of that love, and a result of it.

There is sorrow that is not from God. It is not a sorrow *for* sin. It is a sorrow which *is* sin. This is that sorrow which when given a way to salvation in God, stays where it is. Sometimes it comes under the guise of godly sorrow, but it is not. It is a sorrow used only to draw attention to itself. It is a sorrow sent not to convert, but to destroy.

This kind of sorrow brings first depression and then despair. It brings sickness to the body. It comes forth from the author of death and lies. It is itself a deception. It leads all who hold onto it to a living death. Then to a death that is final.

This kind of sorrow often attacks the saints of God as a deception. It claims to be from God, but it is not. This is a lie. It says this only to find a foothold into our life. Once it takes hold, it is difficult to cast off. The more it grabs hold, the more it demands. The more it demands, the weaker we are to resist. Its goal is to take it all. It is sent from hell and seeks to take us there itself. Anyone who has finally seen through this deception knows that what I say is true. This kind of sorrow is not saving. It is damning. It does not bring an appreciation of God's gift of life. It brings a desire for death.

But there is a way out of this ungodly sorrow. The way out is through thanksgiving and praise. The Scriptures say we enter into God's presence through thanksgiving and praise.

St. Paul always ends his treatments of overcoming vice with virtue with an encouragement to praise. He says to praise and thank God always and for everything in the name of Jesus Christ.

It is hard enough to thank God always, or in the midst of sorrow. How can we thank God for everything, even for our sorrow? How can we thank God for an ungodly sorrow? Do the Scriptures say woe to those who call evil good and good evil?

The Scriptures also say that God causes all things to work together for the good of those who have been called according to God's purpose. God is sovereign. God is in control. God does not cause evil, but God does permit it. Evil is never out of control. God defeats it by using it against itself. Therefore, we can thank God even for the sorrow and tragedies in our life, for even these have a lesson to teach if we but have the eyes and ears of faith with which to perceive. Even as Christ is hidden under the form of bread and wine, or in the poorest of the poor, so too are deeper lessons often hidden under the form of life's tragedies and sorrows.

To praise God this way takes faith. Such praise is not always inspired by feelings. It is a decision. It is a choice. It is an act of the will. In fact, it often goes against our feelings. But once we enter into praise and thanksgiving of God by faith, our feelings will follow. It may take time. Even a long time. But it will happen.

Praise and thanksgiving of this kind are like priming a pump. When a pump is dry, you pour water down a shaft designed to bring water up. You seem to do the opposite of what is needed. But by pouring water down the shaft, you prime the pump and are suddenly able to pump water up to the surface again.

The same is true with overcoming sorrow through praise and thanksgiving. When we are in sorrow or despair, the last thing we feel like doing is praising and thanking God. We are in pain. We are in despair. We do not feel like thanking anyone, especially God, for this sorry condition.

But if we thank and praise God anyway, by faith rather than by feelings, our feelings will soon follow and begin to rise up out of the depths of despair. Suddenly the light of God will break through and we will be able to see things in a whole new light. Ironically, things will not have changed. We will have changed.

It is as if we were on a downward spiral into darkness through sin. This downward spiral of sin leads to death. It starts out through deceptive joy. This false joy gives way to sorrow. Sorrow gives way to despair, and despair gives way to death.

Praise and thanksgiving are able to turn the spiral upward. We may not immediately break into the light. We may have fallen very deep into the darkness indeed. But sooner or later we will break into the light. After that we will rediscover the love, joy, and peace of God that are born of the Spirit and lead to abundant and eternal life.

This praise and thanksgiving stir up the Holy Spirit. It is the Holy Spirit who comforts us in our affliction, mourning, and sorrow. The Spirit has been given in many ways. It has been given in word and in sacrament. It has been given through the brothers and sisters of the Spirit's body on earth, the church. It has been given by humankind, which bears the Spirit's image, even though obscured by sin. Finally, it has been given to all creation that bears the Spirit's traces. The Spirit has been given as a gift to all.

But a gift must be received if it is to be appreciated. God gives the gift of the Spirit. The gift has already been given. The sacraments of the church, especially, give the gift or grace of the Spirit they symbolize. But we must actively reach out to receive the gift if we are fully and consciously to realize its effect in our life.

It is like the birth of a child. Children are given life through the parents by God. Life is a total gift of grace. But as soon as they are born, children have a world of choices ahead of them that very really affect the quality of their lives, and even whether they will live or die.

The same is true with the gift of being reborn by the Spirit of God. The rebirth of the Spirit is a gift of God. It happens to us and for us. But what will we do with this gift? We must respond to it. We must choose to receive it. We must choose to use it. We must choose to stir it up or it will be of no apparent benefit to us. It will sit unused. Like the saying goes: If you don't use it, you will lose it.

This is what praise and thanksgiving do with the Spirit of God. They help to stir it up. To fan it into a full flame from just a tiny spark. This is why some Christians don't really know the full power of the Spirit in their lives. They haven't learned how to receive the gift. They haven't learned how to stir it up. They haven't learned how to enter by faith into praise and thanksgiving to overcome their sorrow.

To learn the secret of praise and thanksgiving does not mean you enter into some kind of automatic joy. God is interested in human response. God does not want us to respond like robots.

Mourning and sorrow do not disappear from our lives once we discover the way of thanksgiving and praise. They simply take on a new meaning. We discover a new way to deal with them so that they are transformed from instruments of darkness and death into pathways to a deeper joy.

Jesus was a man of sorrows and acquainted with grief. He wept over the hard-hearted religiosity of Jerusalem. He wept over the death of his good friend, Lazarus. He wept in the garden of Gethsemane when he faced his own crucifixion and death. These were tears of love. He loved the ancient faith of Jerusalem. He loved his close friend. He even loved his own life, for it was itself a gift of the Father.

Nor was this some cool experience in respectable tears. In the garden of Gethsemane Jesus sweat blood! He had a complete emotional breakdown. It is also okay for us to break down emotionally, as long as we are able to get back up. Sirach says that it is a good thing to grieve when someone close to us dies. He encourages real gut-wrenching grief: to wail and moan! But after a few days he says it is time to carry on. After that this grieving won't do anyone any good. It won't bring back the dead. Nor will it really help us. Grief for a time is good. It is honest. It is real. It is actively healing. But after a while it becomes destructive.

So it is okay for the person of praise and thanksgiving to experience sorrow. To expect our faith in Christ to take all sorrow out of life is unreal. It would rob us of the gift of being human. Jesus restores us to real humanity again. He allows us the blessing of sorrow and mourning, but he also gives us a way to keep them from getting out of control and becoming destructive to our life. In this we find the blessing of godly sorrow and mourning. In this do we find a comfort that is lasting and real.

Finally, mourning does pave the way to meekness. It is only the heart that has been broken that becomes a heart that is truly humble and meek. It has been said that humility can come only through humiliation. Meekness comes through brokenness.

We cannot plan this. It is not a planned spiritual exercise. It happens to us. It happens through life. It happens through love. If seen with the eyes of faith, it is a gift from God.

Once we have received the gift of sorrow and mourning that come from this brokenness, then we cannot help but be gentle and meek with those who are being broken. One is the door to the other. Once we have gone through it, it is almost impossible to go back again. Let us pass now through the door of sorrow and mourning into the blessedness of meekness. Let us go on to the next Beatitude of God's love.

4

"Blessed are the meek, for they will inherit the earth"

JESUS SAYS, "Come unto me, for I am meek and humble of heart." Likewise, some translations of the Scripture list meekness among the fruit of the Spirit. Jesus himself rode triumphantly into Jerusalem to the royal greeting of "Hosanna," riding an ass, a symbol of meekness and humility.

What does it really mean to be meek? Does it mean to be timid and unsure of ourselves? Does it mean to always depend on others to speak or act boldly when the time for action comes? What does meekness mean?

The words used for meekness in Scripture all imply the primary virtue of humility. But there is a different flavor to this humility when found within meekness. According to the definition of the words for meekness, there is an added gentleness to this expression of humility. There is also a very noticeable mildness. This is so strong that some translations actually render the word "gentleness" or "mildness."

In this regard, those who are called to this blessed meekness of Christ are to be a "gentle people." We are to respond to force with gentleness and brutality with mildness. It is this meekness that will teach us how to turn the other cheek and how to be peacemakers in the midst of our often violent world.

But this does not mean we are to be cowards or wimpish. It does not mean that we are to be passive toward the issues that face individual life or our world.

Moses was a man whom the Bible describes as meek. In fact he was called "meek above all men," or "the meekest man on the face of the earth." But this did not mean he did not stand up to the issues God called him to face. He spoke out against the strongest political and military force on earth when he spoke out on behalf of his people before Pharaoh. He led a people through the desert in the face of starvation and war to get to the promised land. He led them as an army against their persecutors. He even faced rebellion and mutiny in the ranks of his own people when the going got tough.

Moses was meek because he relied totally on God for his direction and strength. His first impulse was to pray. Then after hearing the will of God he became a mighty warrior for justice, truth, and the will of the Lord.

Jesus, as the new Moses, was also meek. He might well have taught the blessedness of poverty, meekness, and peacefulness. He might well have turned the other cheek at his own trial and crucifixion. But Jesus was also a fighter. He was not afraid to lift his voice against the hypocrisy of the religious leaders of his day when it was God's will to do so. Some of the fiercest words in Scripture against the hypocrisy of vain religion came from the lips of Christ himself. So meekness did not keep Jesus from being strong in the Spirit of his Father. But it did keep him totally dependent on his Father God.

Perhaps a look into the meaning of humility itself might shed further light here. The root of this word means to be "brought low." Sometimes it can be learned only through humiliation. How true it is that our tendency is to puff up our false self in order to think more highly of ourselves than we ought, and to have others do the same. Sometimes God needs to "burst our bubble" so we can come back to our real self. But sometimes we puff up the false self in egotism because we don't really understand our true self.

The saints have said: Humility is just the truth. Jesus said we will know the truth and the truth will set us free. This is the truth: We are all creatures of God, created in God's image and totally dependent on God for life itself. We are also sinners. We have missed the mark of perfection. Therefore, we are also totally dependent on God for our redemption through Jesus Christ.

But we also need to understand properly this whole notion of sin. Sin means "to miss the mark." It was a word used in archery tournaments when an arrow missed the bull's eye. It did not mean the arrow was necessarily going the wrong direction. Nor did it even mean the arrow completely missed the target. It meant simply that the arrow had missed the balance and perfect centeredness of the bull's eye.

It is much the same with us. Most of us generally seek goodness, truth, and beauty. Most of us want to love and be loved. Most of us even have some sort of belief in God. But we miss the "bull's eye" in all of this.

We remain uncentered. We are imbalanced. We still sin. We need to be redeemed.

Very few people are actually doing a 180° turn on God. Very few people purposefully set out to make war on God. Yes, a few sad and miserable souls engage in such folly as a conscious and willful act. But very few do so intentionally. They do it through omission, laziness, and neglect. It has been said that the world is full of agnostics, but there are really very few, if any, real atheists.

Many people also grossly misunderstand original sin. Original sin is the corporate sin of all humankind, passed down from Adam and Eve through every generation.

Now some have taught that this sin is so radical that it totally eliminates the image of God from the human soul. As we know, human beings were originally created in the image of God. The fullness of that image is lost through sin and restored by being conformed to the image of Christ. But some teach that the image is radically absent from all human beings without faith in Christ. In fact, even after faith in Christ, they teach that the basic tendency of the human being is toward sin, not toward God.

Martin Luther, in trying to describe the mystery of sin and redemption in Christ, taught that sin makes the human soul like a pile of dung. The atonement of Christ is like a layer of pure white snow that covers the dung heap of our lives. While we now look pure to God and to others through the atonement of Christ, beneath the layer of snow we are still a pile of dung.

While Luther's intentions were correct, this understanding has vast ramifications on the Christian outlook on all human life, ramifications that are not good. They are even catastrophic and tragic.

If I really believe that all human beings are essentially a pile of dung, it will radically affect the way I think of myself and the way I treat others. First, if I really believe that I am just a pile of dung, redeemed or not, I will develop a very low image of myself. This will eventually backfire with a vain attempt to come up with a self that has some worth. This results in coming up with a false self, which results in egotism.

Likewise, if I really believe that others are only a pile of dung, I will not treat them with the dignity of human respect. Furthermore, even my Christian efforts to evangelize will easily degenerate into a ministry of numbers, rather than a ministry to precious human souls that bear the image of God.

The effect of this belief is one of the major tragedies of the sociological development of America. Founded primarily as a Protestant nation, it substantially bought into Luther's analogy. Many of our forbearers had this theological footing from which to build their view of basic human self-worth. John Calvin took it even further. Many Catholics did the same through the widespread errors of Jansenism. Consequently, generation after generation were ingrained with a teaching that propagated this extremely low self-image within ourselves and others. After generations of trying to live an ideal that is essentially demoralizing and untrue, we have sprung back with a desperate attempt to establish basic human self-worth.

Unfortunately, this has snapped back in an error of

equal force to the opposite extreme, the error of egotism. Today, Americans are a "me-first" people. We look out for number one. We learn to "assert ourselves" and how to "win through intimidation." This theological error regarding sin and redemption has wreaked havoc through a whole society's understanding of basic human self-worth. It has made us, first, insecure and frightened, and then reactionary in an essential self-centeredness and egotism. John Henry Newman once said that any nation founded on heresy will end in apostasy. I am afraid we have become living proof of the rightness of his saying.

St. Augustine, and St. Bonaventure after him, taught that the human soul is like a mirror created to reflect the image of God. Sin is like dirt that has covered the mirror and kept it from reflecting God's image rightly. Redemption in Christ cleanses our mirror of the dirt of sin. It restores us to our original capacity to reflect God's image in our own human soul. Because there is sin in our world, this is a day-to-day process. It is ongoing.

This analogy does all that Luther was trying to do, but avoids all the theological pitfalls and errors. It recognizes the reality of sin and the need for redemption. But it never takes away the soul's potentiality for reflecting the image of God. Hence, the soul never loses godly respect.

This changes the way we think about ourselves. It changes the way we think about others. It causes us to treat all human souls with the reverence and respect of a vessel that bears within itself the potential to reflect the image of God. It maintains an appropriately good self-image and keeps us from abusing ourselves or others. Furthermore, within Christian ministries, it keeps us from ever treating a precious human soul as just another "pile of dung" to be covered with the snow of Christ. It keeps us from treating them as just another number chalked up in winning the world for Christ.

It is the truth of creation, sin, and redemption that causes us to be truly humble and meek. St. Francis says that what we are before God, that we are and nothing else. This means that all the good we have from God is real. Sin is also real. Likewise, redemption is real. Therefore, we are to be confident in the good we are, repentant and contrite for our sin, and grateful in our redemption. It all comes from God except sin. That came from Satan and human pride. To deny any of it would be untrue. It would, in effect, deny the saving work of God, and this would be actually to deny God.

This all leads to the truth of human interdependence. All humankind reflects the image of God. The church manifests the body of Christ himself. All of us are interdependent with one another.

St. Paul says that the church is the body of Christ. Like any body, it has many members. Each member, by the nature of the body, must work in interdependence with the other to accomplish common tasks. Therefore, we need each other. Each member must be competent to fulfill its role, but no one task can be accomplished by one member working independently of another. They must work together, no matter how competent any one member may be at its task.

Likewise, the successes and failures of one affect all. If any member suffers, the whole body suffers. If one member is in pain or is not functioning properly, the other members must compensate. If they cannot, then they must suffer loss with the weakened member, even though they themselves may be strong. The same holds true for success. The brilliance of one member's function might bring success to all, even though some members may be weak in and of themselves. The body is a unit of interdependent members. To deny this is to deny the essential reality of the church.

The same could be said for the whole human family. We all bear God's image. We have all been given a particular talent and gift. If we want to be open to God's full grace, then we must be open to the gift and grace of every human soul. This necessitates some real humility.

This is illustrated even in secular government. If a good government is in control, all prosper. If a bad government reigns, all suffer. Likewise with economics, if one succeeds, it gives employment and blessing to all. If one fails, others are somewhat deprived. Whether Christian or not, believers in God or not, all humankind is interdependent. This is the plan of God. It is a fact of creation.

This means there must be an appropriate humility before each other. St. Paul says we are to consider all others as superior to ourselves. Does this mean we have no gifts? Of course not! It simply means that every human soul has a gift that we do not have.

No one member of the human family or the body of Christ has it all. We, in turn, have a gift that no one else has. This brings an attitude of reverence and humility before all, each according to our own position. We are humble before all humankind, for we are humble before a bearer of the image of God. We are humble before every member of the church, because we are humble before a bearer of the Spirit of Christ.

There are two abuses of interdependence prevalent in America today. Independence and codependence. Independence is a denial of our dependency on God and our interdependence with all humankind, the church, and all creation. It is often a reaction to a low self-image that leads to undue individualism and egotism. In the end it alienates us from all people, the church, and all creation.

Codependence is an undue dependence on people, the church, or the created world. It, too, comes from a low self-image that tries to find itself in another person or created thing. It leads to an unhealthy love-hate relationship, for when you find that no other person or thing can really give you a lasting sense of identity, you will grow disillusioned, frustrated, and eventually come to hate of the person or thing you once loved too much. This hate will eventually lead to despair.

Both independence and codependence are perversions of interdependence. Both are born of an unhealthy low self-image. Both lead to alienation and despair. Both come from the author of lies and are designed to lead us into a living hell. Only the truth of God, creation, and redemption through Christ can set us free. This truth is utter dependence on God and healthy interdependence with other people.

There is one last aspect to the truth of humility. It has to do with humility before all creation. Both St. Augustine and St. Bonaventure say that all humankind bears the image of God, the church reflects the body of Christ, and all creation bears God's traces. God's image is more

exalted than God's traces, but God's traces upon anything are enough for us to give reverence and honor to
that thing.

It is said that St. Francis could see the traces of
Christ's footprints before him in all creation. Because
of this he became a saint who authored the Canticle
of the Creatures and the greatest nature mystic of all
Christendom. Today, the church calls him the patron
saint of ecology.

Others in the church have also unlocked this mystery
of creation. Thomas à Kempis says in his *Imitation of
Christ* that if our hearts were pure then all of creation
would appear for us as a book of holy doctrine. It would
teach us the mysteries of the reign of God.

Paul says that the invisible realities of God are clearly
manifested to all humankind, even without the Law,
and can be recognized through the things God has
made. So important is the creation that Jesus died on
a cross to reconcile not only sinful human beings, but
all creation as well. He says that all creation waits for
the manifestation of the redeemed sons and daughters
of God so that it will be released from the bondage of
human sin.

Finally, Jesus, the founder and author of the whole
church, saw the messages of God coming through every
aspect of the created world, human and nonhuman, an-
imate and inanimate. The bulk of his teachings came
from the birds of the air, the lilies of the field, or the
grain of wheat. He says that if human beings do not
cry out "Hosanna" to him and his reign, even the rocks
will cry out.

This is hardly a tradition that does not see value in

the created world. Ironically, much of Christianity has failed to recognize this heritage. Some have said that Christian industrialism has been responsible for most of our ecological havoc. Ideally, we should be humble before every aspect of creation, for it all bears God's traces. We should treat it with reverence. We should treat it with care.

Furthermore, there is a very real interdependence with all creation that should be respected. Jesus says God causes the rain to fall or the sun to shine on the just and the unjust. We are all affected by the seeming moods and shifts of nature.

If the weather is good we are all blessed. If it is bad, we all suffer. The drought reduces all humankind, despite all our technological advancements, to trepidation and fear. The hurricane, the tornado, the volcano, the earthquake, all affect even the most "independent" and "secure" of persons, organizations, or nations.

It is sheer arrogance to think we are somehow above this interdependence. To consider oneself independent of such an awesome force is foolhardy at best. Likewise, to become too dependent on creation, no matter how beautiful it may be in bearing God's traces, is to rob ourselves of real dependency on God and God alone.

But it is also true that creation is interdependent with us. If we sin, creation is kept in bondage. If we are redeemed, it is redeemed as well. Whether we like it or not, God has put us into the garden of creation to be its stewards. How well we steward has tangible and sometimes terrible effects.

Today we can see the results of our bad stewardship. We have not been humble. We have often been arrogant. We have not been responsible, we have been irresponsible. Somehow we thought that we could take from creation whatever we wanted, destroy whatever we wanted, and dump wherever we wanted, and there would be no result. The time has come to pay the piper. We have danced to the tune without a care. Now it is time to pay.

This can be seen in many ways. Irresponsible industry has polluted air and water. The imbalances of agribusiness have upset the natural cycles of soil, rivers, and air, not to mention the natural balances in healthy food and plant and tree production and distribution. The whole planet is in jeopardy and stands on the brink of ecological chaos. Ozone is running out. Oxygen is running out. Water tables are being depleted. Weather is erratic and extreme. Truly, all creation groans.

Ultimately, however, it is people who suffer. These imbalances cause sickness — sickness in mind and sickness in body. They cause pain, suffering, and despair. In the end they can even cause death.

The planet earth is a small planet. Its resources are not inexhaustible. It cannot absorb unlimited abuses. It is like a spaceship that is flying us all through space. It is like a lifeboat in an endless sea. If the spaceship is destroyed we will all perish in outer darkness. If the lifeboat sinks we will all be left to drown.

It is up to those who really walk in the humility and meekness of Christ to see that this does not happen. It was Moses' humility and meekness that allowed him to answer God's call and lead the chosen people out of bondage. It is our entering into the humility and meekness of Christ that could enable us to lead not only the new sons and daughters of God, but all creation, out of its present bondage to sin.

Of course, nearly all of what has been said could apply to a humility based on logic and logic alone. Real meekness adds a whole new dimension to humility. It adds gentleness. It adds mildness. The primary reason for this is the tenderness that comes from love.

Here we inherit all the earth and respond to it out of love. We interrelate with others humbly, not only out of logic, but also out of love. This means we are gentle and mild. Why? Because love treats others the way we would wish to be treated ourselves. Most of us prefer gentleness to brutality and mildness to harshness. Our humility before others is truly meek when we have discovered the mildness and gentleness of love.

The same is true regarding all creation. When it has been raped by humankind out of arrogance, greed, and lust, we desire to calm it with the humility and meekness that comes from love. Likewise, when we interrelate with creation, we seek to move it with the gentleness of a lover. Only those who know this genuine meekness will be given the blessing of all the earth by God.

So, like Moses, we are to deal with the issues that face our world. But if we are followers of Jesus, we cannot respond from the pure logic of justice and peaceful coexistence. We must respond in love. This will make us like Jesus himself, "meek and humble of heart." Then will we inherit the earth. Then will we know the blessing of God.

5

"Blessed are they who hunger and thirst for righteousness, for they shall be satisfied"

HUNGERING AND THIRSTING ARE STRONG IMAGES. Of the basic needs for human existence listed in Scripture, food is mentioned first. Food and drink are, indeed, basic needs to live on planet earth. Without them we die.

If you have ever been to the Third World you see hunger and thirst in a way that leaves an indelible image on your soul. You never forget the eyes of the starving. It has been said that there are four reasons for death in the poorest nations of the world: bad food, bad water; and no food, no water. Most killing sickness and diseases in Third World countries come from bad water. You never forget once you have seen mothers give their children contaminated water because there is simply no other water to give.

When we hunger and thirst we are compelled. Our pursuit becomes all-consuming. It is all you can think

71

about. It is all we can do to stay rational. We force ourselves to stay rational in order to stay alive. But we are
consumed with hunger and thirst for the same reason.
Our life is at stake.

Perhaps this is why Scripture is full of the analogy
of hunger and thirst to describe our desire for God. The
Psalmist says that our longing for God is like a deer
that yearns for running streams. A soul without God
is described as parched land in the desert. The prophet
Isaiah encourages those who do not have money to buy
food and drink to come to God, for God will become
their spiritual food and drink.

Jesus calls himself the food and drink for those who
hunger and thirst for God. He calls himself the bread
of life that comes down from heaven. His flesh is real
food. His blood is real drink. He says that he will send
the Spirit from the Father, and this will be for us like
living water that springs up without ever running dry.
This same Spirit working through the church says to all
who are thirsty, come and take the free gift of this water
of life. Finally, we are promised that in heaven we will
never again hunger, that we will never again thirst. All
of our hunger and thirst will be completely satisfied.

Our hunger and thirst can be satisfied only by God.
St. Augustine said to God, "My heart is restless until
it rests in you." It has been said that there is a space
inside the human soul that can be filled only by God.
Until that space is filled, we are incomplete. All our life
we try to fill that space with ideas, people, and things,
but we are left unfulfilled. Only God can fill that space.

While the metaphysical facts of this analogy may or
may not be accurate, they do describe the reality of the

human condition without God. The human soul has been created in the image of God. It, therefore, has an innate desire for the things of God. The human soul has been created to seek after goodness, truth, and beauty. The human soul seeks after love. We want to love and be loved. Even when the soul looks for these things away from God, it is looking for God. God is the source of all these things. They, in turn, must lead back to God when approached with the eyes of faith.

Even sin cannot totally keep the human soul from reflecting God. Sin has no creative force of its own. It can only pervert. Only God can create. What God creates is good. Therefore, sin can only be the perversion or abuse of a good thing. When we are in sin, many times we are still looking for God. We just don't know it yet!

In the eyes of faith, even sin will lead us back to God. Lust is only a perversion of love. Abuse is a perversion of use. Greed is a perversion of stewardship. Every sinful appetite is really only a perversion. Ugliness is a perversion of beauty, and error is a perversion of truth. Even Satan himself is a perversion of the greatest of all archangels in heaven. In the eyes of faith, we find God even through these sins by looking past the perversive power to the truly creative power. That power is God. With this understanding in God we are able to defeat the devil with his strongest tool: sin.

All of this is said only to point out that all creation hungers and thirsts for God. The creature seeks the Creator. Humanity hungers and thirsts for the divine. Even when creation is perverted and abused through sin, it still manifests the human longing for the things of God. It has simply gone wrong. If we can point things in the right direction again, even the worst of sinners will find their deepest longings fully satisfied in God.

Jesus blesses not only those who hunger and thirst. He blesses those who hunger and thirst for righteousness. But what does righteousness really mean?

The Greek word for righteousness can mean many things. It quite literally means "rightness." To seek the right. It also means "equity." To seek an equality among all. This implies "justice." It is justice that brings peace.

Righteousness often stands in stark opposition to the values of the world. In this self-centered society of ours, people aren't always interested in doing the "right thing." The rampant materialism of the West comes nowhere close to the private ownership with equality spoken of by the early church. The justice that brings peace is found neither in our domestic court system, nor in our dealings with other peoples and nations.

It is justice that helps to being peace. When the poor are being continually oppressed and abused by the rich, the poor will eventually rise up to overthrow their oppressors. It may take time. It may not happen until there is a sufficient number of the poor. But it will happen.

Unfortunately, this overthrow usually involves violence. While the church supports the rights of a people to take up arms to establish or defend their basic human rights, it encourages the avoidance of any use of violence whenever possible.

How much better it would be if the people who do the oppressing simply chose the way of justice, equity, and rightness voluntarily. In the long run it would actually head off the violence bound to be done even to themselves. It would work to the benefit of the poor. It would work for the benefit of the rich as well. It would work for the benefit of all.

This equality does not mean all will be identical. Not all people desire the exact same set of clothes, or the same house or car. Not all do the same kind of work, or enjoy the same kind of pleasure. Equality must be lived out with a real respect for human diversity.

Equity in sacrifices is not identical either. A seemingly small sacrifice by a poor man may mean more to him than a rather large one by someone who is rich. Or conversely, a small austerity by one who is accustomed to a life of leisurely plenty may mean more than a more substantial austerity to one who is accustomed to such things through a life of poverty. Equality is not just a matter of mathematics. The whole human person must be considered.

It must be remembered that this righteousness is not human in its origin or accomplishment. It comes from God. In a very real way it is God's righteousness we seek. It cannot be established on our own.

This is seen most clearly in Christ. He lived this rightness, this equity, and this justice as a gift from God to all humankind. He is righteousness incarnate.

He also accomplished God's righteousness for all humankind on the cross. All humankind had sinned and fallen short of the glory of God. Humankind was headed toward death. Jesus bore that death on the cross. As perfect and true man, he could bear someone's death other than his own. As infinite and true God, he could bear the death of all humankind and all creation as well. In this he paid the debt of justice through his death so that new life could be freely given as a gift to all.

The church is like a child playing ball by the street. The child has been told by her parents not to chase the ball into the street because of the dangerous traffic. This is a law based on love. But when the ball rolls into the street, the child runs out into the traffic anyway. When the father sees a car speeding toward his child, he runs into the street himself, knocks the child to safety, but is hit by the car himself. The child is saved through the sacrifice of the father.

So is the justice of the cross of Jesus. We were told not to sin because it would bring death. We did it anyway. When God saw death approaching, God sent Jesus into the world.

Jesus knocked us out of the way of the death we deserved and bore it himself. Because of sin someone had to die. Because of love it was Jesus rather than us.

This is how God accomplished righteousness and justice for us, and then made it a free gift to us. This is how God robbed the justice of death through death. Praise God, death cannot defeat the author of life. Jesus rose from the dead to prove once and for all that the victory had been won!

Another rendering of the word "righteousness" is "holiness." The Scriptures are filled with admonitions to be holy. Be holy for I am holy, says the Lord. But what does holiness mean?

Some popular teachers have defined holiness as "wholeness." True enough, one more obscure meaning has to do with being "one thing" or "whole."

How desperately the world needs the wholeness of holiness today. Both people and society have been fractured into a thousand pieces. Ironically, when the world seems smaller than ever before through modern transportation and mass media, global injustice, poverty, and war threaten to tear the world apart more than ever before. When there are more means available for inner healing through spiritual, psychological, and emotional health than ever before, churches, families, and individuals are falling apart through abuse and stress.

People are more self-centered than ever before, yet no one seems able really to come to self-fulfillment. We emphasize self-enlightenment, yet remain in the dark. We talk about healing constantly, yet our world is still desperately ill.

Something has gone wrong. We talk about wholeness constantly. We claim it as our right. We use our inability to find it in ourselves as an excuse for our inability really to help others. We are so busy trying to be whole that we end up fracturing others. We are so busy trying to get healed that most of the world continues in sickness and pain.

Jesus is our only source of wholeness. He is the healer. If we want to be healed, we must get our eyes off ourselves and onto Christ. Otherwise our desire for wholeness isn't holy at all. It is just self-centered.

Jesus says we find ourselves by losing ourselves. He says, further, that the gift we have received must be given away. Likewise, if we want to be healed ourselves, we must concentrate on healing others. If we want to be whole inwardly, we must sometimes turn outward. We must turn to Jesus and then to people.

The real healing that brings wholeness comes out of love. Love cannot center on itself. If it centers on self, it is not love at all. It is only egotism.

But love of self is part of the Christian message. Jesus says we are to love others as we love ourselves. No doubt, the intent of these words is to show the importance of loving another. It was taken for granted that people love themselves.

But in our modern time self-hatred has become a very real problem. As we said earlier, this is the result of a theological error that swept America in its early days. As a reaction and result of this error, people have become preoccupied with self to discover who they really are. We have become a whole generation of self-centered people.

Egotism is only a reaction to self-doubt and self-hate. Self-hate produces artificial self-love. Low self-esteem produces artificial self-confidence. Consequently, we have become a people torn apart by each extreme. We have become fractured. We need to be made whole again. We need to be holy.

This is done by returning to a proper self-love. We were created in God's image. God is love. Therefore, we are essentially lovable lovers. Furthermore, we are therefore worth a lot! We bear the image of God.

When we sinned, God loved us enough to offer his only Son to redeem us. Jesus loved us enough to shed his own blood for us. If God loves us, then we must be lovable. Likewise, it makes us worth a lot. Jesus paid his life blood for our soul!

To deny the lovability of our soul is to deny God's love. To deny the worth of our own human soul is to deny the value of God. Actually, to deny our own self-worth or to enter into self-hate is a subtle form of egotism and pride. It denies God. To deny God is the ultimate expression of pride.

One of the greatest expressions of love is forgiveness. Forgiveness brings reconciliation. Reconciliation brings healing. And healing brings wholeness. This happens within human society. It happens within the church. It also happens between humanity and creation. In each case the fragmented and opposing parts are reconciled and brought together into a fully integrated whole. This is the holiness that happens through forgiveness and love. But in order to forgive, we must repent. In order to repent, we must admit there is a problem. So we need to own up to the fractured condition of our soul, our church, and our world. Then we can forgive ourselves and others. Then we can be healed. Then we can be whole. Then we can be holy.

The standard definition of holiness means to be "set apart," to be separate, to be "consecrated." God is holy because God is transcendent, wholly "other." The people of God are holy because they are to be separate from the rest of the world. So the "wholeness" of holiness reconciles us with ourselves and all the world, while the "separateness" of holiness calls us to be set apart from the world.

This separateness comes from a radical following of Christ. If we seek justice when the world seeks injustice, peace when the world seeks war, or forgiveness when the world seeks vengeance, we will be different. If we seek life, if we are pro-life, when the world seeks death through choice, we will be different. We will be like a city set on a hill that cannot be hidden. We will be a light in the midst of the darkness. This separateness is holy.

We cannot do this alone. We need the help of others. If we try to do it alone we will fail. We will fall. The power of the world will overcome us. We must walk hand in hand with our brothers and sisters in Christ so that when we fall, and each one of us eventually will, there will be someone there to lift us back up. To walk hand in hand requires forgiveness and reconciliation. It requires healing of division. This means we, the body of Christ, must be whole. We must be holy if we are to stand the tide of this world. Then will we be able really to share the light of Christ in the darkness of the world.

So we are called to be separate from all in order to be united to all. Likewise, we must be united before we can really be separate and stand against the tide. Real holiness demands that we live in this paradox. While we still sojourn on the face of this earth, we are to be in the world, but not of it. We have been satisfied, yet are still awaiting to be satisfied. We are redeemed, yet still awaiting redemption. We taste of holiness in Christ now, but we still hunger and thirst for heaven.

6

"Blessed are the merciful, for they will obtain mercy"

JESUS SAYS that mercy in the heart is better than the sacrifice of the Law. Likewise, he says that those who scrupulously perform the ritual sacrifices of the Law often miss the weightier matters of the Law: justice, mercy, and faithfulness. It is not unfair to agree with the words put onto the lips of Jesus in a contemporary movie: "The heart of the Law is mercy."

Many times we think of justice and mercy as opposing ideas. Justice demands equality. Therefore it demands payment. Mercy forgives the debt. Is justice without mercy? Is there need for justice once we discover mercy? Are justice and mercy opposing ideas?

First, we must understand that God gave us the law of justice out of mercy. The ancient world was lawless and cruel. The codes of law that existed were often brutal and filled with vengeance. If a personal crime was committed by a member of one tribe against a member of another tribe, often tribal war would result. If a member of one family sinned against a member of another family, the whole offended family would war against the family of the offender. If an individual committed a small crime, death was often the punishment. At the time of the Law in the Hebrew Bible, the "justice" that reigned upon the Middle Eastern earth was filled with brutality, vengeance, and widespread death.

The giving of the Law was to bring a true justice into the world. It was itself an act of mercy. The heart of the Law was "an eye for an eye, and a tooth for a tooth." While this might sound primitive and cruel to us, it was a statement of mercy to the ancient Middle Eastern world. It said that vengeance, cruelty, and unequal retribution against innocent tribes, families, and individual human life were themselves sins against God, the creator of all human life. It was a law of moderation. It was a law of mercy.

It was also mercy because it taught what was wrong and what was right. In the Garden of Eden humankind had claimed to know good and evil, right and wrong, without the help of God. Because of this all of human-kind was deprived the paradise of God where God's truth brought real and lasting freedom. Without God's truth to guide our decisions, the whole human race fell into bondage. Without God's light we fell into darkness, despair, and death.

The Law was God's attempt to show us this truth again. God even wrote it down for us to see very clearly. Some believe God even wrote the most essential part, the Ten Commandments, with God's own divine finger, without the help of human vessels. What does this Law do?

It shows us the truth again. It gets us back on track. It takes us for our errors in judgment and leads us back to the way of God's truth. This is not the act of some cold and legalistic God. This is itself an act of mercy.

It is like a train and a track. The engine is full of power. The coaches are comfortable. The dining car is equipped with the best of food. But if this train has no track to guide it, it will not reach its destination. All the preparation will be in vain. If it goes off the track once it has begun, it will wreck, tragically. Many lives can be lost.

The same is true with humankind and God's law of justice. We might have the best of intentions, and we might even be quite comfortable with our own judgment about what is right and what is wrong. But without God's Law to guide us about real justice, all of our good intentions and intellectual training will be in vain. We will not reach our desired destination. We will not travel the proper course, and we will miss our goal. In fact, we might end up in a huge "train wreck" where many human lives are lost.

Whether in the Hebrew Bible or the New Testament this principle remains true. Jesus says that not one crossed "t" or dotted "i" of the Law will be changed until the full coming of God's reign, and that if we change it we will not be doing the will of God. He says that his followers will fulfill the Law even more completely than the scribes and Pharisees. But we must not fulfill only its external legalities. We must fulfill its original intention of mercy and love for all humanity. Then we will more than fulfill its external dimensions with the right motives: the motives of mercy and love.

In the time of Christ the observance of the Law had degenerated into mere external observance. The internal motives of mercy and love had largely disappeared. Instead of a truth that set people free, it had itself become and bondage. Instead of lifting them out of sin, it had ground them deeper and deeper into the guilt of constant condemnation. The ones who did the condemning were not any freer than the ones whom they condemned. The whole system accomplished the opposite of its intent: the happiness and joy of being free from a life of sin.

Jesus came to return us to that original intention and to help us reach that goal. He said that we will know the truth and the truth will set us free. What is this truth? He says that he, himself, is the way, the truth, and the life. He feels free to amend the Law in the Sermon on the Mount because he is the Law. He is the Word made flesh.

In the Hebrew Bible God sent us, as it were, a letter. He sent us the Law. It was very much from him. The words were written by God. But it still remained just a letter. It was written by one who was still far away. The letter of the Law was definitely from God. But it was not the same as having God say it in person.

In Jesus, God came on a personal visit. Jesus was the Word incarnate. He lived what was written. No longer was it a matter of mere words on a page. In Jesus the Law took on flesh. It had a body, soul, and a spirit. It was now fully alive, and alive in a way that human beings could fully understand. There was no danger of misinterpreting the letter. He was living it out for all to see. He could interpret it for us. He could even amend it as humankind developed further into time and matured as it grew older so that it could better achieve its desired purpose. He was, after all, the one who sent the old letter in the first place.

It is not unlike us if we were the god of an insect — say, ants. The ant colony had turned away from our loving guidance. We sent them communication from a distance, but they still didn't get it right. Finally, we made the supreme sacrifice of love. We actually gave up the developments and blessings of our humanity and became an ant in order to save ants. We became like them in all things, except their disobedience, so they could fully understand what we were trying to say. The same could be said about Jesus' incarnation. He gave up his heavenly dwelling and became a human being in order to be understood by human beings. He became one of us to save us all.

Jesus does amend the Law of the Hebrew Bible. He fulfills it, but goes far beyond its minimal requirements. He takes us far beyond the danger of mere external observance into the real interior motivations of the Law: justice, mercy, and faithfulness. He takes us back to the heart of the Law, which is mercy.

Jesus says that we have heard it said one way by the teachers of the Law of old. But now he says something new as the Giver of the Law. We have heard it said about the externals of adultery, divorce, oaths, or retaliation. We have heard the moderate minimums about anger, lust, and vengeance. Now he is going to tell us something new. He is going to take us deeper. He is going to take us further.

He cuts right to the heart of the old Law when he says

that the eye for the eye and the tooth for the tooth is now going to become something new. The eye for the eye and the tooth for the tooth had served as the moderating minimum against vengeance and anger throughout the Hebrew Bible. Now it was being surpassed. It was being amended. It was being changed.

Jesus says that now we are to turn the other cheek. We are not even to resist injury. We are only to pray. He practices what he preaches in the garden of Gethsemane when he says to Peter when Peter tried to defend Jesus' unjust arrest: "Put away your sword. He who lives by the sword will die by the sword."

Jesus teaches us and shows us a new and higher way: Violence just begets more violence. Judgment begets judgment. Justice begets justice. The problem is that we do not always judge with God's judgment. We do not all view equity and justice with the higher perspective of God. Therefore, even when seeking justice, the cycle of violence continues.

We can break the cycle of violence only through nonviolence and nonresistance. We can break the cycle of misguided human justice only with God's unconditional mercy.

But what does mercy really mean? It means to be compassionate. It means to be sympathetic. But it also means much more than sympathy. It means to empathize. Empathy means actually to "get inside" the other person. To see things from another's perspective before we judge another too harshly from ours. To understand another's motives, as well as to perceive that person's actions. This radically changes the way we bring "justice" to others. As a native American Indian saying goes:

"Before you judge another person, walk a mile in that person's moccasins." Or as the 1960s song went: "Walk a mile in my shoes."

If we empathize with other people, it will radically affect our perception of justice and judgment. They might well be "criminal" from an external perspective. But if we look inside we might find their motives were correct. They might have been seeking the "equity" and "rightness" of godly justice. But they may have failed in their attempt to carry it out. They may have misunderstood certain principles and laws through ignorance. Likewise, they may have been sidetracked through another human sin that fouled up the purity of their original undertaking. All of this must be taken into account.

Of course, today we have a situation different from the one that faced the Jesus Christ of history. We face a different problem.

In our day it is difficult for mercy to build on justice because we have lost even the basic sense of justice. It is difficult for love to build on the Law because our society has become so lawless. It is difficult to forgive sins when the society no longer even knows there is such a thing as sin.

From our experience in community, we find that most American Christians no longer have a sense of justice or responsibility or commitment. People do not expect to be held accountable for anything. They take responsibility for nothing. They just float from place to place, community to community, and relationship to relationship — expecting to be "forgiven" by God's "mercy." This, too, is a grave abuse of Jesus' original intent.

Ironically, the Christian message must once more

proclaim the Law so that the fullness of love may have some substance and meaning. We must once more preach justice so that forgiveness will have some meaning. We must teach the basics of the truth and hold our brothers and sisters into accountability. Then will things like forgiveness, compassion, and mercy not just be excuses for lawlessness.

How did our society get into this mess? It is much the same as what I said earlier about sin. The faith of our forbearers overemphasized the Law. It overly externalized the Christian and monotheistic concepts of righteousness and justice. This led to extreme rigidity. Rigidity led to unfair judgment of others — the exact opposite of Jesus' intent.

As a reaction to this abuse, we came forth with an emphasis on mercy and forgiveness. This emphasis led to overemphasis. Use led to abuse. Reaction gave birth to reaction. What was needed was response.

There is a difference between reaction and response. Response meets an abuse with strong, loving, and deliberate use. It brings extremes back to the moderate. It is well thought out and confident. It brings the far left and right back to the balance of the center.

Reaction meets abuse with an opposite abuse. It meets extreme with extreme. It is not well thought out, but meets a crisis with the proverbial "knee jerk" response. It is not confident, only cocky. Not strong, but forceful. It does not bring people, ideas, or things back to a balanced center, but jerks and whips them around to the opposite extreme.

This is, in my opinion, what occurred with the law and mercy within our society in the last hundred or so years. Mercy came forth, not as a response, but as a reaction. What was needed was response. What was left was an overly permissive society where all concepts of justice, equity and right were gone. Civil courts degenerated into a system where criminals were protected and the law-abiding citizen went on trial. Self-centeredness became the norm for all society. Forgiveness and mercy were expected, so all felt free to get away with whatever they could, with only a minimal price to pay.

This "me-first" expectation of mercy is not what Jesus had in mind. It is essentially self-centered and presumptuous. It is eating away the basic fabric of our society. It destroys families. It destroys the work force. It destroys the quality of the products we produce, if not the quality of our whole way of life. It destroys our civil system of law and justice. Soon it will destroy our whole way of life, if it has not done so already.

The Scriptures say it is presumption to expect forgiveness without real repentance. Likewise, we are not to use mercy and forgiveness as a cloak for sin and unrighteousness. Forgiveness and mercy from God and others is a grace, it is not a right. If we are serious about turning back to God we will repent, we will seriously change our way of life. Then will the mercy and forgiveness of God and others have some credibility. Then will it accomplish its original intention and goal: the freedom of sinners from the bondage of sin.

Mercy and forgiveness are like rain that constantly falls from the sky. It is constantly offered by God. Our life is like a cup or glass left out in the yard upside down. In order to get "filled up" with God's grace of mercy

and forgiveness, we must turn ourselves rightside up.
We must change.

So it is with forgiveness and justice. In order for us to
activate God's mercy and forgiveness, we must change.
We must turn ourselves "rightside up." We must turn toward God. To demand that God or others fill us up with
living water when we refuse to turn ourselves rightside up is presumption and self-centered pride. Furthermore, it is just plain stupid. It is the mercy of God that
first teaches that the cup must be turned rightside up before it can collect the living water of forgiveness. It is also
the mercy of God that rains this living water constantly
upon the earth. It is up to us how we will respond.

This is the practice of "tough love." It means allowing people to take full responsibility for their actions
in order to teach them the responsibility of real love.
It means allowing them to bear the consequence of
their wrongdoings in order to teach them the wrong-
ness of sin. Likewise, it lets them suffer firsthand the
consequences their own sin often brings to others. Real
love — love of neighbor and a healthy self-love — does
not knowingly seek to bring this kind of suffering into
the world. Tough love allows people to taste just enough
of the consequences of their own wrongdoings to consciously turn around from their sin. It encourages them
to change. It does not, however, let them suffer to the
point of death or permanent harm. Nor does it enjoy
watching the learner experience pain. It does this so the
learner will properly live. The Scriptures say that the father who loves his son will chastise and discipline him.
He does this so that he will grow up knowing what is
right and wrong, and why it is right and wrong. He does

this so that his son might grow up to prosper and live. Tough love does the same. It is an expression of mercy.

So the church of today's modern world has a double challenge: to preach the law of justice and the grace of mercy. It must firmly establish, or re-establish, the truth of God's justice that will set all humankind free, and then mercifully forgive all who fail to live up to this high ideal. The church must set its face like flint against the tide of modern, overly permissive fads and opinions when they are wrong, yet its heart must remain compassionate and soft toward all God's children.

It is not unlike the analogy of the sheep and the shepherd. A good shepherd must use the rod and the staff. The rod pushes the slow ones forward when they lag behind. The staff pulls back the ones who are going too far out ahead. Both keep the sheep from being where they should not be. The use of the rod and staff might seem a little "uncomfortable" at the time. But it keeps the sheep on course. It gets them to greener pastures. When exercised by a good shepherd, it is done out of genuine concern and love.

Of course, this is not to negate the importance of mercy and forgiveness. It has been said that peace must build on justice. But who is really just in God's eyes? Scripture says there is not a just person left, not even one. If we wait for justice to bring peace, we will wait forever. It is only mercy and forgiveness that will break the cycle of brutal violence and hard-hearted judgment. It is only mercy that really paves the way to lasting peace.

Ultimately, it is Jesus and Jesus alone who is the example and fulfillment of God's mercy. It is Jesus who comes into this world to manifest the living Law, the

Word incarnate. It is Jesus who takes on human flesh in order to empathize with all humankind. It is Jesus who fulfills all the justice of the Law even to the point of martyrdom at the hands of the Law in order to release those who were in bondage to the Law. It is Jesus who shows us a mercy that is not just a good idea. It is love.

We can learn one of the greatest lessons about mercy from Jesus's parable of the merciless official. In this parable the official is forgiven a just debt by his employer. Yet the official will not forgive the just debts of those employed by him. Even though the debts are just, the merciless official is condemned as an act of justice. Why? Because he did not show others the mercy that had been shown to him.

All we really have to do to be inspired about being merciful with others is to look at how merciful the Lord has been with us. As Paul says, forgive as the Lord has forgiven you. Yes, we may outwardly fulfill the demands of justice most of the time. But what about the times we have not? Furthermore, what about the attitudes behind our actions? I am afraid that no one, including us, is just in the eyes of God. It is actually an act of justice to show mercy to others.

Really, in the end which is easier? To keep driving someone deeper into guilt by demanding justice, or simply letting that person go through mercy? The goal is to get the person freed up from sin. Sometimes this happens better through forgiveness than through justice. When the mercy of justice has failed time and time again, try a little of the mercy of forgiveness. You may find it works better. Love gave us the Law, but as Scripture says, love covers a multitude of sins.

7

"Blessed are the pure in heart, for they shall see God"

THE NEW COVENANT IS A MATTER OF THE HEART. The prophets say that the New Covenant will actually be written on the heart. Our hearts of stone will be turned to hearts of flesh again. The divine gift will make us fully human again.

The prophets say that the human heart is deceitful beyond all things and beyond cure. Only God can search the heart fully. The Psalmist says that only God can cleanse us of our sin and create a clean heart for us again.

The Psalmist also says that only the pure of heart may climb the mountain of the Lord and stand in his holy place. David himself is said to be a man after God's own heart.

Jesus reaffirms this emphasis on the heart in the Beatitudes. Jesus says it is not those who are clean outside through ceremonial observance and ritual who are clean before God. The heart must be cleansed. It is from the heart that come the greater evils: evil thoughts, unchastity, theft, murder, adultery, greed, malice, deceit, licentiousness, envy, blasphemy, arrogance, folly. It does little to clean and purify our external, religious observance without first purifying the depths of the human heart.

The Sermon on the Mount elaborates on this Beatitude and cuts to the heart of all sin. Here Jesus teaches about adultery and divorce, but first teaches about adultery in the heart. He teaches about retaliation by speaking about anger and love. He teaches about oaths by encouraging us really to understand the heart or meaning of our simple words. In all these things he deals with the external sin by getting to the real heart of the problem. The issue is purity of heart.

But what does purity of heart really mean? The Greek word used here for pure, *katharas*, can mean many things. But all of them are helpful for our understanding of the term and have an essential unity in meaning.

First, the word can mean "clean." In this sense, it was used primarily of "cleaning" corn or grain by winnowing or sifting it. In this process the chaff, or unusable part of the plant, is separated from the pure grain, which is usable for food and nourishment. Winnowing is done by throwing both the grain and the chaff up into the air and letting them fall so that both wind and gravity separate them naturally.

The word was also used for purging an army of its bad soldiers. Those who frequently complained and performed badly were purged by their superior from the ranks before a major battle so that the army would be "clean." The purging might have meant smaller numbers, but it also meant greater strength.

This word was also used to describe metal that had been purified by fire to separate the impure and weak metal from the pure and strong. It could also relate to other substances such as milk or wine that were not mixed with water, but were pure, rich, and strong.

We can see why some translations render "purity of heart" as "clean of heart," or "single-hearted." It means a heart that is totally unmixed in its motives. It is interested in God and God alone.

We can also see that purity of heart does not come automatically or passively. It involves action. It involves vulnerability in the face of another's action and the choice to take action of our own. Sometimes it involves pain. Some of this action involves getting thrown around a bit. It is like the winnowing of grain. Both grain and chaff feel a little helpless and out of control when they are mid-point in the air. The fall to the ground can be a little frightening and painful. But it accomplishes good in the end.

Purity of heart can also involve the purge of separating ourselves from activities, places, and even people who are mixing up our hearts. Purging a bad soldier is like letting go an employee. It is never easy, but sometimes it must be done. It is never easy to "let go" of sin and the things that are taking us away from God. But in the end we find our hearts undivided and centered wholly on God. This way is usually a choice on our part.

Finally, purity of heart can involve the trial by fire that actually burns away the wood, hay, and stubble of our life from the precious metal of our heart. In the process we often think we are going to die from the pain or that we are living in a hell on earth. But the purging fire actually comes from the love of God to purify us and make us strong. In the end we become both more resolute never to go through the fire again unless absolutely necessary, and more compassionate with those who are still in the midst of the flames. This purging is usually done to us by God through circumstances beyond our control It is rarely a matter of choice. It is a matter of acceptance.

We could spend much time looking at the areas of impurity of heart mentioned in the Sermon on the Mount: sexual impurity, anger, judgment, or religious hypocrisy. Each of these areas could easily demand a chapter, and we all know these problems plague us today just as much as they plagued people in the times of Christ. Suffice it to say that these impurities still divide the house of our individual heart and our church and our world today, and leave us dangerously vulnerable to being fully conquered by the enemy, the devil and his angels, when left unchecked and ignored.

I would rather touch on some positive principles that help to unite the heart in Christ and Christ alone. The first is this: if you want to stop doing the don'ts, get busy doing the dos. If you spend your time doing the dos, you simply won't have time to do the don'ts. There are so many challenges that face the true disciples of Jesus in this world. If you face even just a few of them, believe me, it will demand so much of your time in positive things, you simply won't have time for the negative.

Along the same lines, it has been said that if you want to discover where your heart is, see where your mind goes when it wanders. If it habitually goes to sin, then your heart is divided. If it goes to God and God's purposes, then your heart is single and pure.

One of the ways to control the mind is by good Christian meditation. This means taking the time intentionally to fill our minds and thoughts with the ways of Jesus Christ. This is done by meditation on the Scriptures, or solid and trustworthy devotional practices. These are all aimed at turning the mind to Christ in an intentional and disciplined way.

When we do this as an intentional discipline, we discover that our thoughts will soon begin going to Jesus on their own in their wanderings. Once we train the mind to take this journey through intentional discipline, it will begin doing it on its own by way of habit after a while. It will become almost second nature.

These recommendations will begin to rechannel or program both our thoughts and our actions in a way that substantially purifies our hearts almost naturally if practiced diligently. If we fill our lives and our thoughts with the good, the bad will be displaced almost naturally.

It is like a glass filled with water and oil. The more water we put into the glass, the more the oil is simply displaced. The glass isn't big enough to be filled with both at the same time. If we fill the glass of our lives with God and God alone, we will simply displace the things that are not of God. Then our hearts will no longer be divided.

But sometimes no matter how hard we try to do and think only good things to purify our hearts, bad things keep invading with relentless persistence. Sometimes we simply do not feel like doing the work of Christ or thinking about God. Sometimes even when we want to, we simply seem unable.

This is when it is important to remember that faith is a choice. Love is a decision. Many times we will not feel like doing the work of God, or meditating on God. This is precisely the time we must do so! As we said earlier, life of faith is like a chain. It is only as strong as its weakest link. Likewise, it is when we don't feel like doing God's work or meditation that we must do so by faith. Then we will find out how strong our faith really is, and we will strengthen that faith by our work and meditation. Furthermore, we will discover that the whole chain is stronger and can accomplish far more than one isolated link.

This is not to say that our feelings should never be involved. God created us with emotions and feelings. God wants to redeem them and use them. A life of faith is not, however, guided by feelings. It is guided by a decision of faith. Where our faith is there our feelings will follow.

Jesus says that where our treasure is there will our hearts be also. If we choose to make the decision of faith our treasure, our heart will follow. We may not feel like doing God's work or filling our thoughts with God all the time. But if we do so by a decision of faith, then sooner or later our feelings will follow. Our hearts will be purified.

Again, it is like priming a pump. When the well has run dry, we must prime the pump in order to get the water flowing again. At first, this might seem to be quite unnatural. We must actually pour water down a shaft created to pump water up. At first it seems artificial and contrived. It seems to be the opposite of what is needed. But in the end it causes water to flow freely from the depths of the earth.

Likewise, we must prime the pump of purity of heart through a decision of faith. At first our hearts might not feel faithful at all. But if we act on the decision of faith in God, our hearts will follow. It will be purified.

Sometimes, however, these feelings don't follow very quickly. Sometimes it feels like they won't follow at all! But if we continue in faith, the feelings will follow. It may take days or weeks. It may even take months or years. But God will reward our decision of faith with eventual feelings of spiritual consolation. We may have to enter the dark night of the soul. But do not be deceived. This dark night will not stay forever. Our life is a constant flow and alternation between faith and feelings, between trial and reward. It is precisely this process that purified our hearts like precious metal in fire. The fire is the love of God. The precious metal is our hearts.

It is much like the experience of walking across a great continent on foot. The continent is made up of hills and valleys, mountains and desert. From a distance it is the variety that makes the continent seem so beautiful. But close up, the desert and the wilderness seem endless to cross on foot. It is only the experienced traveller and real nature lover who learn to see their beauty close up.

Likewise with our spiritual life. From a distance both the fertile plain of the charismatic and the desert of the contemplative dark night seem beautiful. But when we are in their midst, they can seem endless, ho-hum, or harsh. The variety is there for the faithful traveller.

But the inexperienced will often lose heart in the difficult times and give up, or grow infatuated in the good times and not proceed further. Only the experienced traveller knows to keep going in order to experience it all and to see even the beauty of the difficult desert or wilderness of the Spirit even at close range.

Know, too, that some of the greatest purifications of our hearts happen without us knowing it at all. We think we have struggled and failed, that we have travelled without reward. We think we have failed the test of fire. All we are aware of is the resulting burn. But deep down inside, God has done a secret work. God has purified our hearts. This is actually the greatest purification of all.

As Jesus says, this is like the farmer who buries seed in the earth. Although the farmer does not know how it happens at all, the seed sprouts forth into young plants that grow and produce much fruit. Likewise, sometimes we feel buried in the ground. We feel like we are suffocating, like we are being buried alive. Finally, we have no choice but just to let go and die. Then, without knowing how or why, we are resurrected as we sprout new life and come into the sunlight again. As the popular verse says, it is when we see only one set of footprints in the sand that Jesus was actually carrying us. We were never alone at all.

Of course, there is a unique aspect to this Beatitude that we cannot overlook. This is the only Beatitude that speaks of "seeing God." This is revolutionary, for Middle Easterners believed that no one could see the face of God and live. Only those like Moses and Elijah were granted this privilege, and then only in partial ways.

Now Jesus is opening up a whole new dimension to the human experience of union with God. But even in the era of the Christian church, full vision of God is reserved for heaven. It is "already" and "not yet." So is it for now or later? Is it a promise of heaven, or can we "see God" even while on earth?

Seeing God does begin here on earth by looking through the glass of creation. Thomas à Kempis says that if our hearts were pure, all of creation would become a book of holy doctrine for us. Likewise, Bonaventure says that all creation bears the traces of God. In a very real sense, the pure of heart are able to see God through God's traces in creation. Without purity of heart this all escapes us.

Bonaventure also says that if our vision is pure, we can see God's image in other human beings. In a very real way this enables us to see God's face in the faces of all people. Yes, their faces may get dirty through sin from time to time, but their faces can always be washed clean. Then their faces become a most pure reflection of the face of God.

Furthermore, the Scriptures are the written word of God. According to Middle Eastern understanding, the word is the extension of the soul. Therefore, the Scriptures are a written account of the actual soul of God. If our hearts are pure, then the Scriptures take on a whole new importance and dynamism in seeing God.

The same could be said of the sacraments. They symbolize and effect the grace of God. If our hearts are pure, the sacraments become a conscious and lived experience. It is no longer some secret workings of God on the soul of the half-hearted recipient. When our hearts

are pure, we can put our whole heart and soul into the
sacraments so we can fully receive their grace in a conscious way. We "see God" in what is only vain and
empty ritual for many.

But as dynamic and effective as all these may be in
revealing God, they are not God. God's face may be
traced or reflected in creation and humanity, but they
are not God's face. God's heart or soul might be revealed in Sacred Scripture, but it is not his soul. Jesus
might be really present under the form of bread and
wine in the extraordinary sacrament of Eucharist, but
it is not his pure, uncreated presence. It is still hidden
under the form of created elements. We still see bread
and wine. We do not see God's uncreated essence. God
uses these means as tools to draw us to God. But in
the full sense of the word, they are not God. They are
only God's tools. They are gifts from God. But they
are not the fullness of the Giver. They are only God's
gifts. In one sense, God's face remains veiled through
God's revelation in these things. In another sense, for
the pure in heart God's face is unveiled through these
things.

The full image of God is beyond description. God's
face is beyond being seen. Yet for the pure of heart, it can
be known. It must be seen with the heart. It is beyond
the perception of the eyes. It must be perceived with
the heart. It is beyond being understood by the mind.
It must be known by the heart. Yet it remains beyond
full knowing.

To know God in this way is like being expanded to the
far left and the far right in an instant. It is like breaking
through to eternity for a moment. It is as if blinders

have been taken off the perception of our souls, and suddenly we can see.

I call this the experience of "falling up." It is like our souls being pulled, as if falling, out of the created world into the realms of the Eternal. It causes us to gasp and our hearts to both speed up and slow down. Yet our physical heartbeat remains the same. Our souls seem to explode and disintegrate so they can be scattered to the far reaches of Eternity. It is much like dying, but it brings us more abundant life.

It is the experience of paradox at its fullest, yet it remains true. God is the Alpha and Omega. God is the first and the last. God is eternal; present in the past, present, and future all at once. When we break through to this vision, our souls know this paradoxical aspect of God as a flash of experience. Our souls seem to explode and disintegrate so they can be scattered to the far reaches of Eternity. We know all, yet can explain nothing. We hear the first and last words of God, yet can say nothing. We see everything, yet remain in the dark when asked to describe the light we have seen. If we try to explain it, it eludes us. If we try to speak it, we lose it. If we try to describe it, our words stumble and fall. The word we hear can be spoken only in sighs or breaths. The extreme motion through the Eternal can be maintained only in absolute stillness.

Once we have had this experience we feel as if we have actually died and come back to life. We do not want to come back, but we must. If we stayed in this state, we would surely die. If we stayed, we would have to pass on to things that simply could not be continued in our present human condition. We have to go on or come back. We cannot consciously be there and here in this state at the same time. If we stay in the Eternal, we must die and go on. Once we come back we are no longer afraid to die. We are ready, almost anxious, to go on. But we also begin to live on earth with a whole new effectiveness. We are better for it. We are, in a sense, reborn.

I suppose at the time of death we will simply go to this place and stay there. We will not come back. We will go on. To go there prematurely would be a mistake. Not to go at the proper time would be tragic. There is more than we can ever conceptualize on the other side of death. Much growth is required before we go. Much will surely follow. I believe this is what we call purgatory. For believers it burns away all imperfections in a flash that seems both an eternity and an instant. This is a fire of divine love. It expands us. It causes us to explode and seemingly be destroyed. But it causes us truly to be what God has created us to be in the Eternal.

All this comes together in Jesus. He is the Creator and the created. He is the Incarnation and the Ascension. He is now both with a body and omnipresent throughout all Eternity at once. As some of the great Christian mystics said, he is both the center and the circumference, the center that is everywhere, the circumference, nowhere. He is the ultimate paradox. The ultimate mystery. He is the cosmic Christ. Fully God, fully human, to reach humans and make them divine in himself. He is life in death, eternity in time, God in humanity, yet without losing the fullness of either. This is beyond human words. It is communicated only in the word of the God-

Man. It can only be spoken in the present reality and being of Jesus Christ.

Of course, this latter experience is nothing to be toyed with. It is not a game. It is reality — and an explosive reality at that! If we force or manipulate our way into this experience, great psychological and spiritual harm could result. It is important first to learn to see God's face in the more ordinary means given to us by God through creation and the church before such extraordinary experiences are a possibility for us. Even for those well-grounded in the faith, such experiences can leave one psychologically and spiritually vulnerable for a while. For the inexperienced they could bring both deception and disaster. The experience could even end in death. It is important to be well-grounded in our faith in Christ and to be guided by someone older and wiser in the Christian faith to help us keep our balance when such things become a part of our experience in Christ. Most importantly, we must center this experience on Jesus and Jesus alone, so that we will not be deceived by a false psychological or spiritual experience that leads not to purity of heart, but to impurity and pride.

This experience of seeing the face of God often leaves us a bit shaken. But when it is genuine, the opposite is eventually true. When our souls are incinerated in the fire of God's gaze, we seem to disperse across all creation in a sort of smoke, like that which rises from holy incense. Then we gently fall back to the earth to become more fully one with all things and to help enrich the earth for the production of new life. We bring a sweet smell to all. Far from "falling up" so that we can never come down again, or falling in one disastrous crash, we are gently dispersed to all the earth again. But now, instead of belonging only to ourselves or to just a few, we belong to all.

It is not unlike the example of lightning and light bulbs. The flash of lightning is powerful enough to light up a city. It is exciting and inspiring. It almost defies description. But unless its energy is harnessed and channeled into electric light bulbs it is useless. In fact, it can be harmful and destructive. The light bulb might seem dull in comparison to the lightning, but it is the light bulb, not the lightning, that effectively brings light to the city of God in practical and useable ways. The mystical rapture of "falling up" is like lightning. It is exciting and inspirational. But its incredible power must be transformed into light bulbs so it can give light to others in a practical way. True mystics who have seen the face of God will, like Moses, veil the shining of their own faces so others might truly benefit from their own mystical union with God.

Finally, as we consider all of this in light of the beatific idea of purity of heart, we do well to reconsider the ancient Middle Eastern concept of the human heart. For the ancient Middle Easterner the heart was the center of the soul. It was the center of the whole human being.

When Jesus and all the Scriptures speak of a pure heart, they are really referring to the whole of human life. Jesus tells us to purify the very center of our being by putting him there. When Jesus becomes the absolute center of our whole life, then, and only then, will our heart be truly saved. When he who is utterly simple and whole is at the center of our lives, then we become truly single-hearted. When he who alone is clean comes to the center, then our hearts will be clean. When we put Jesus at the center, our hearts will be pure.

8

"Blessed are the peacemakers, for they will be called the children of God"

IT HAS BEEN SAID that there can be no peace without justice. But it has also been said that no one is just in the eyes of God. Therefore, peace can only come through forgiveness.

Jesus was speaking to an audience torn with strife. They were living under Roman occupation as a conquered people. Various groups existed within the Jewish ranks who put forward their ideas about justice and peace for Israel. Typically, these groups were also divided from one another. So the division and strife continued. Sometimes it even broke out into violence.

The Jewish sects spoken of in Scripture shed some light on these divisions. They can also teach us something about our own. The Pharisees were the spiritualists of the day. They believed in the spirit world and the afterlife and looked to the eternal realms for lasting peace. The Sadducees were the rationalists. They did not believe in the spirit world or in the afterlife, so they tried to bring peace in the here and now. But they did so through careful diplomacy and political maneuvering. The Zealots were the fundamentalists of the day. God said it, they believed it, that settled it. God said Israel would be a nation, so they were ready to fight in any way to re-establish it, including going to war with Rome. All three groups included aspects of truth, but they were divided among themselves as to how to bring justice and peace to Israel. Probably a little of all three would have worked best.

Today we still have Pharisees, Sadducees, and Zealots. They simply go by other names. The Zealots are the peace and social justice activists. They are always ready to protest, to rescue, or even to take up arms in the name of justice and peace. Their zeal is good, but it usually needs to be directed and moderated. The Sadducees are the theologians and prelates of the church. They must develop the rationale of a problem and solution and bring this idea before the church and civil leaders. Their rationale is good, but it also needs a little fire and empowerment by the simple action of the Spirit. The Pharisees are the charismatics and other renewal groups in the church. They are always ready to spiritualize a problem in our world. There is a demon under every rock. The simple word of God in the Bible is always the answer. And the final solution is always in heaven. While these approaches are all to some extent true, a little common sense and action in the here and now would help while we all sojourn on the face of this earth. All three have something to learn from one another.

Let us now consider the first statement: There can be no peace without justice. We too have our oppressors and our Roman Empire. We too have our injustices, our inequalities, and our abuses. Likewise, we also have not just three, but a myriad of mutually exclusive sects and special interest groups, ready to put forward their ideas as a way to the justice that leads to peace.

I would like to begin from where I am: A Catholic Christian perspective. I must say with all humility, and yet with boldness, that I have never seen any institution, secular or religious, so ready to meet the issues of our modern world with a developed yet uncompromised grasp of the gospel of Jesus Christ and a truth that is consistent and even. I have never seen a "Declaration of Independence" as true as the gospel. I have never seen a Constitution or Bill of Rights as consistent and developed as the Second Vatican Council and the ensuing papal encyclicals. No, they are not without problems and are in need of further development. But all things being equal, I have never seen anything on earth to match them.

Let us start by reviewing much of what has been said above, in particular the Beatitude concerning poverty and wealth. We reached the conclusion that private property might be retained, but only with real equality between the rich and the poor. The church teaches the same. It says that while private property is a basic human right, all property retains an essentially communitarian or social character and purpose. This holds true for all people, Christian or not. Thus, the Christian community itself should strive to function under a socioeconomic model that is essentially communitarian and social. Since the Christian is called to overflow from a primary focus on the church and the heavenly reign to all the world, some political involvement and social participation is in order.

Government is the primary structure of society. Without it there is chaos. Even primitive tribes have a council and a chief. If the Christian is interested in bringing justice and peace to those who are not yet Christians, political movement is appropriate and even necessary by some. It is an act of pre-evangelization. It is an act of sharing the good news we have found about our way of life with others. It is not perfect. It will never replace the full expression of the church or God's heavenly reign, but it is good as far it goes.

The church has spoken clearly against the abuses of the two major approaches to political ideology in our world today. One is atheistic Marxism. The other is materialistic capitalism. Atheistic Marxism is wrong in its denial of religious freedom and the right to personal property. Capitalism is wrong in its embrace of godless materialism and consumerism and its military in defending these errors. Both represent an extreme. Both try to spread their errors to the rest of the world through imperialism.

The church teaches a way that stands between the two. It is the way of democratic socialism. While the church itself is careful to point out that it is not directly advocating any one political solution to injustice in the world, the final translation of its teachings into the political arena by the qualified laity in its ranks is at least some political form of the socioeconomic system of democratic socialism.

The signs of the times show us that this is the direction of the future. The recent revolution in eastern Europe or the attempted revolution in China show us that communistic Marxism does not seem to work. It doesn't meet basic human needs and rights. Likewise, the continued revolution in Central and South America against American-backed capitalist dictatorships shows the same. The poor have a right to some form of equality. The world's oppressed are rising up.

A change is in the wind. It is a change that has vast ramifications. It affects the whole world. It affects the future of our planet. Christians have a responsibility to be on the cutting edge of that movement. We, above all others, have a solution to the world's problems. Our church has taught and presented these solutions for a long time. Now it is time for us to implement them in a tangible way.

But we must be careful about jumping too quickly onto the secular band wagon. No existing political solutions fully embody the teaching of the church on justice and basic human rights. Here in America, neither the Democratic or Republican solutions offer anything we can fully support. Even the newly emerging Democratic Socialism is at odds with some fundamental church teachings about the human rights of the unborn or the consistent reverencing of human life.

Only the church offers an option that is fully consistent. This option is the consistent life ethic. It protects basic human rights from the process of conception to death, and even through eternity. Contrary to Democrats and socialists, the church teaches against artificial birth control and abortion. Contrary to Republicans and capitalists, it teaches that the truly just government and society should help provide and maintain basic human rights to food, clothing, shelter, health care, education, and employment. Contrary to communistic Marxism, it maintains private property, freedom to choose a vocation, freedom to raise and plan a family, and freedom to worship God in the religion of one's choice as basic human rights. The church stands in contrast to any one of these existing political options.

There are two ways we could still participate. The first is to compromise. The second is to idealize. Either way we must eventually actualize.

Compromise means working with the existing group that is most consistent with the issue closest to us, and working from there to bring change. If it is pro-life vs. abortion, you might be a Republican. If it is concern for the poor and disarmament, you might be a Democrat. If it is equality with privacy, you might be a Socialist. All of these are compromises, and no one of them is truly consistent even with the issue they champion, but at least it is a start. It is a step in the right direction.

To idealize is to start something new. Imagine if all 50 million Catholics in America united behind these issues. Imagine if all 850 million united throughout the world. We would be one of the largest nations on earth. Plus, imagine those who would join us from the other like-minded Christian and monotheistic religions, not to mention all people, both religious and nonreligious, who agree with the consistent life ethic. We would be a force to be reckoned with. But the force would be only a force for life. It would be a force of love.

All of what has been said above about justice and basic human rights applies to every level of human society. It affects personal relationships. It affects life in the church. It affects social and political life in our secular world. It even affects our relationship to nature. Each level of human existence is interdependent with the other. While the emphasis on the church and the reign of heaven remains primary for the Christian, we all are affected and have an effect on every other level. It is the principle of a justice that upholds a consistent life ethic and the protection of basic human rights that helps to bring an enduring peace to any one of these levels.

Justice must be built before we can expect peace. When there is injustice there is social unrest. Social unrest leads to violence and war. If we want to bring lasting peace, we must first establish justice.

But who is really just in God's eyes? Who is really just in the eyes of our fellow human beings?

I am very much involved in the struggles of various parts of the world. One such area is the Middle East. I am always amazed at the Middle Eastern capacity to remember the sins of past generations. Dialogue for justice and peace becomes a touchy exercise in diplomacy between two extremes when each is outraged at the injustices shown toward it by the other side. These injustices often go back many generations.

While these injustices are real, and I have reached a personal conclusion about where the greater injustices lie, I am convinced more than ever that peace will come only when both sides are willing to forgive and forget.

There comes a time to bury the hatchet. There comes a time to forgive.

So we can also say that peace comes only through forgiveness. If we spend all our time trying to even out the score through justice, we will never have peace. No one is fully just in God's eyes. There comes a time to simply tear up the scorecard and start over. There comes a time to give each other a clean slate.

This is essentially the way of peace taught by Jesus. He said we must be willing to forgive anyone who shows even the first signs of repentance. We must be willing to do this repeatedly. Yes, we should work for justice, but we should never expect that anyone will ever be totally just. We must always be ready to forgive.

Jesus also teaches us the greatest way of non-resistance. He says that if anyone slaps you on one cheek, you should offer the other as well. In the Middle East of Jesus' day, this meant being prepared, not only to be unjustly insulted, but to die without offering resistance. St. James indicates that the early Christians did this when he says that the rich oppress the poor and the just, but the poor do not resist. Likewise, the early church fathers indicate that this way of nonresistance was practiced at great cost even by those in the Roman military who became followers of Christ.

This is the most radical way to bring peace. Simply refuse to fight. Break the cycle of violence. Show the way of peace at all costs by example. It may not seem to work at first, but in the end it has deeper and longer-lasting results.

This does not mean we are not to raise our voices against injustice and violence. Jesus cried loudly against the hypocrisy of the scribes and the Pharisees. He taught the way of peace. We do well to lift our voices against the religious and secular evils of this world in imitation of Christ. But we do better to follow him to the foot of the cross. He had said what he had to say. All knew it well. Now it was time simply to do what he said. It was time to practice what he preached. He preached non-resistance and peace. Now he had to break the cycle of violence, war, and death by his own death without offering resistance or stirring up more violence. It seemed to be the way of defeat, but it led to victory. It seemed simply to allow injustice and violence, but it brought the civilized world to a whole new level of justice and peace. Christendom may have been far from perfect, but it did bring a level of justice and peace to the civilized world it had never seen before.

Today, we are called to do the same. We may well be called to speak out and demonstrate for justice. But we are also called to speak out and demonstrate for peace. We are called to bring the development of world justice and peace to a level it may never have seen before.

This means we enter into a kind of passive resistance. We stand up for justice, but we refuse to use violence. We are willing to suffer so that others might be healed. I would point out, however, that Jesus did not really teach either "passivism" nor passive resistance. He taught and practiced nonresistance. He was not passive. He was active. Neither did he resist. He was nonresistant.

We will search in vain to find an example of Jesus demonstrating against the oppressive occupation of the Jewish people by the Roman Empire. If anything, he seems almost disinterested. The early church continued with an attitude that was similar. This is true even when Jesus, Peter, and Paul all die at the hands of Roman injustice; yet they never seem much concerned about civil government.

Jesus, Peter, and Paul concerned themselves primarily with the reign of God. They kept their eyes on a peace that is within, a peace that is eternal — a peace that really lasts. Perhaps this is for one essential reason: How can you give what you do not possess? How can the church dare speak of peace to the governments of the world when it is still so divided within its own ranks? How can we try to bring peace and justice to the church when we do not yet have the justice and peace of Christ within our own souls? Jesus taught us to concentrate first on these things. Peter and Paul found that to do so took up their entire lives.

9

"Blessed are those who are persecuted for the sake of righteousness, for theirs is the kingdom of heaven"

IF WE TRY to live the other seven Beatitudes, we will not only be different from the rest of the world. We will be persecuted. If we try to live the blessedness of poverty of spirit, we will be persecuted by the rich. If we live the blessedness of godly sorrow, we will be resisted by those who want only to see happiness and joy all the time. If we are meek and humble, we will be persecuted by the powerful and proud. If we seek to live in righteousness and justice, we will be persecuted by those who live in unrighteousness and propagate injustice. If we try to be merciful, we will be persecuted by the unmerciful. And if we try to bring peace onto the face of the earth, we will be persecuted by those who prosper and gain by keeping the world at war.

Jesus never said we wouldn't be persecuted. He only said we would find blessing. He might well have said we would receive the hundredfold blessing on earth and in the world to come. But he also promised persecution. Christians will be persecuted. They always have been. They always will be. Jesus' way is the only way for his true followers. That way is the way of the cross.

It is like being the new kid on the block. When you first arrive you are tested. Sometimes you are even persecuted. This is because you are different. People make fun of the things they don't understand. This mocking can easily become persecution. Jesus is the new kid on the block of the world. He was mocked. He was resisted. He was persecuted unto death. Christians too remain new to the world. Our ideas are revolutionary. Our ways are different. We can expect to be mocked, resisted, and persecuted. Sometimes, this persecution will be unto death.

But there is another persecution: Being ignored. As the new kid is slowly integrated into the neighborhood, the other children learn that the easiest way to deal with his difference is simply to ignore him. He isn't going to go away. Neither are they. A stand-off remains.

We could easily say this has developed between Christianity and the world. Christianity wouldn't go away so it was simply absorbed into society. Its more radical message was ignored. Popes, bishops, and Christian leaders are often invited to speak to various world leaders and organizations, but their essential message is politely ignored. We too are passively accepted and politely treated as respectable members of society, but this essential and radical dimension of the Christian message remains unheeded. Simply to be ignored can be a persecution worse than death.

Personally, I have always found some persecution whenever I seriously decided to follow Jesus. When I decided to follow Jesus and actually call myself a Christian, I was persecuted and ignored by some of my old friends. When I decided to become a Catholic and follow a monastic way of life, I was resisted and persecuted by some other Christians. When I reformed the community I founded back to the fire of its original vision and zeal, I was persecuted by other "religious." When I heard the Lord calling me to marriage as my wife and I gave birth to this community, I was resisted and persecuted by some who had made a god out of celibacy. Each of these decisions was duly discerned in the church as the following of Jesus' call, and each decision has borne good spiritual fruit a hundredfold. Yet each decision stirred up at least some persecution. And the persecution was sometimes intense. It has been said that if you are not stirring up at least some persecution then you probably aren't really following Jesus radically. If it doesn't shake the nest a little, perhaps it isn't really worth doing.

Ironically, the persecution we face often comes from other Christians. It often comes from those we love the most. Since we often are no longer the minority in the midst of a firmly established non-Christian religious institution, we face the scribes and Pharisees from within. We must face scribes and Pharisees — Jesus did! So God allows us to face the scribes and Pharisees within Christianity itself. God knows there is plenty of "religiosity" within organized Christianity. If viewed with faith, this mystery actually becomes a grace. It allows us to be more like Christ.

But sometimes we are the scribes and Pharisees.

Sometimes we do the persecuting without realizing it. This happens especially when we are placed in some kind of leadership capacity. We try to help our brothers and sisters, but we end up hurting them instead. We try to do good, but we do badly. We try to follow Jesus, but like Peter we deny the Lord instead.

This is part of the mystery of redemption by Christ. Jesus allows us to follow his way to the cross fully, even within the church. We are not always understood. Sometimes we are even resisted and persecuted. And sometimes this is done by those we would least expect. It is done by our loved ones and friends.

This is not to say we shouldn't try our best not to be scribes and Pharisees. The fact that we sometimes will be, whether we like it or not, does not mean we shouldn't strive to our fullest not to be a scribe or Pharisee to our brothers and sisters. We should always try to be Jesus and only Jesus to everyone we meet. Remember, the scribes and Pharisees were the "religious" who crucified Jesus, and it was Jesus' "friend," Judas, who betrayed him. We should never respond passively when we find we are betraying and crucifying Christ through our ill treatment of our brothers and sisters. We should repent.

There is also a sort of persecution in failure. Much of what has been said in this book challenges the essential upbringing and sociological conditioning of being an American. At the time of this writing, I am not entirely convinced that Christians in America can overcome this social conditioning and fully follow Jesus Christ. I am not so sure that we are not really more American than we are Christian. Are we American Christians, or Christians in America? American Catholics or Catholics in America?

This is seen in our obvious continuance in materialism, even after a continual call from God through the church to repent. The same could be said for our self-centeredness or our extreme individualism. It most certainly holds true for our approach to sexuality. Finally, it holds true even in the form of government we pledge ourselves to. We don't necessarily want to be this way, but we most certainly are. Somehow we just seem unable to pull ourselves free from the strong current of the American way of life. In all of this I am afraid we continue to be more American than Christian. Our actions speak louder than our words.

We have personally gone through this struggle in our own community where we have tried to live out the above approach to the Beatitudes. We have most assuredly been blessed a hundredfold. God has worked a miracle. God has done more than we could possibly expect or imagine. But we still see an essential struggle between our ingrained Americanism and our Christianity. No matter how hard we try, the struggle remains.

It is hard for materialistic people to begin to live gospel poverty in simplicity. It is hard for "me-first" individualists to live in deference to the will of another in obedience to community. It is hard for those from loose sexual backgrounds to begin living in chastity. It is hard to be an alternative society within the overall secular society.

Furthermore, there is the bottom-line question that faces all societies: What about making ends meet financially? Ideally, this Christian socialism and communitarian way of life based on the gospel should cause the whole community to prosper. But here we come face to face with our own American laziness.

The American work force is no longer putting out better quality and more quantity because of a selfless approach to work and service. No! We expect higher wages and less work. Consequently, the rest of the world, in particular the Far East, is passing us by. We consider ourselves the masters of the world, the leaders in industry, but the rest of the world is passing us by. We have become a debtor nation. Our own cities and land are being bought out from under us by those who are more successful. The reason? Laziness and pride.

In a community such as ours this translates into jobs being done slowly and poorly. It translates into people always ready to claim their right to "pray," even if it means others have to double their work and burn out. It means we want to do things "my way" rather than following the directions of a superior, while still remaining unable really to direct ourselves. It means that what should be done with more efficiency and quality out of a Christian sense of self-sacrifice and service are often done poorly or left undone entirely. Why? We are still more American than we are Christian.

This glaring fact hurts us all. It is a sort of persecution from within. It comes from right down deep inside. It comes from our own souls. It comes from our own guts. It comes from ourselves. As the saying goes: We have met the enemy, and it is us. This fact glares at us constantly in Christian community.

At the time of this writing, this "persecution" scares me perhaps more than any other. I am convinced that the world desperately needs a Christian revolution in order to survive humanly. But I am also convinced that we must first live what we preach before our words will have any real meaning whatsoever. If we are going to change the world, we must first change our own lives. If we are going to change society, we must first come up with our own Christian society that can provide an example to the world. That is what our community is all about. If we cannot make our own lives work, how can we expect to change the world? If we cannot make Christian community work, where do we get the authority to speak? Christianity either works or it doesn't. Christianity has become a religion of words. Now it is time for action. As we say here in our community: Just do it!

But Jesus says persecution of any kind actually blesses us. It is actually a grace. It helps in living out our redemption. Why? Of course, we could point out the scriptural example that persecution and trial are like fire that makes silver and gold more pure. Therefore, they are good. They strengthen our faith. They purify our motives and our actions from the "dross" of the world.

It could be pointed out that our faith is only as strong as its weakest point. Persecution and trial help us to discover the weak points in our faith. They also help to make them stronger once the weakness is discovered.

But there is a more mystical blessing that comes with persecution. It is a blessing based on love. It is the blessing of the cross.

Scripture says that no greater love has anyone than to lay down one's life for a friend. The cross is the place where Jesus laid down his life for us. The cross is the greatest expression of God's love for all humankind.

The cross of Jesus was a direct result of persecution by all humanity. Jesus was persecuted by the religious leaders of his day. He was persecuted by the crowds that hailed him as their king one day and called out for his crucifixion the next. He was persecuted by the cold and insensitive injustice of the Roman civil law. He was even persecuted by his own disciples and apostles who, all but Mary, a few women, and John, betrayed, abandoned, and denied him. There is no persecution we now face that Jesus has not also at least tasted in his own death. All of this persecution led Jesus to die alone on the cross.

The cross is also the place of paradox. It is the place of opposites. It defeats any particular curse by willingly embracing the curse itself out of love. It defeats a thing by the use of a thing out of love. In this, death is defeated by embracing death. Isolation is defeated by embracing solitude. Poverty is defeated by becoming naked, abandoned, and poor. Finally, persecution is defeated by embracing the persecution by all out of love for all. This is the death that leads to resurrection.

This means that the things we used to run from we now willingly embrace. The things we tried to escape because they brought pain to ourselves, we now embrace because they bring comfort to others. We do this out of love for others, even when it is they who nail us to the cross. This brings real freedom. When we no longer run from the power of persecution we are free. Instead of living in fear, we are now really free to love without counting the cost.

Lastly, and most importantly, we do it out of our love for Jesus. We love Jesus. Therefore, we want to follow him. We want to imitate him. We want to embrace him whom we love by being conformed as much as possible to the pattern of his life. This means embracing the persecution of his cross. This means being conformed to the pattern of his death. This is the ultimate act of love.

So we see that these persecutions no longer become something to be afraid of. They are to be accepted. They are to be embraced. The persecutions will come. They have been promised. It does no good to run.

Yes, they will hurt. Jesus wept in the garden of Gethsemane. First, he emotionally broke down. He sweat drops of blood. On the cross he bled further, was crowned with thorns, pierced with nail and spear. He suffocated, his heart burst, and he died. But he remained faithful and so broke through to the blessings of resurrection.

We too will surely experience pain in persecution. But if we embrace the pain out of love for Jesus, love for others, and even love for ourselves, then the pain will be transformed. It will become our comfort. A true miracle will take place and we will be healed. This is the blessing of persecution.

Conclusion

In summary we can see that the way of the Beatitudes is the way of revolution. It changes our whole way of life from the inside out. It starts as an attitude, but it ends as an action. It is an "attitude" that must eventually "be." That is one reason these essential teachings of Jesus are called the "Beatitudes."

As we have seen, these attitudes begin with inner poverty, brokenness, and meekness, and work their way on out to justice, purity, mercy, and peacemaking. They affect the way we think. They affect the way we act. They affect the things in our lives that are deeply personal and private. They also affect our social life with others. This includes Christians and non-Christians. They help us to bring examples of this revolution into the church and the world through the new communities being continually raised up by the Spirit as alternative societies within society. They help us to bring this revolution to all the nations on the earth. Lastly, they keep us headed toward heaven by their mystical character that can never be fully realized in the externals of our lives as pilgrims and strangers on planet earth.

Let us end by taking an overview of the progressive attitudes these Beatitudes bring. We begin with a poverty of spirit that becomes the foundation upon which all the others must build. Then we experience a sorrow and mourning that brings a brokenness into our souls. This makes the mild and gentle humility of meekness possible, which in turn begins to revolutionize every aspect of life on earth. It makes us pliable to the righteousness of God's direction and truth when we have gone astray into error. It learns to see this direction as mercy, but also learns to be forgiving and merciful with others, even as God has been forgiving and merciful with us. This helps cleanse our heart from anger and lust, and brings peace and vision of God to our souls. From this we overflow in loving peace to the world. Lastly, we find both the faith and the love to keep going even in the face of unspeakable odds and persecution through the cross of Jesus Christ.

This is the blessing of the Beatitudes. It is a blessing no human being can take away. It transforms the curses and troubles of this world into challenges and blessings. It becomes the heart of our faith. It is the most important teaching of Jesus.